VULNERABILITY & COMMUNITY

VULNERABILITY & COMMUNITY
Meditations on the Spiritual Life

GARY CHARTIER

Griffin & Lash, Publishers
Ann Arbor, Michigan

Copyright © Gary Chartier 2015

Published by
Griffin & Lash, Publishers
Ann Arbor, Michigan

Vulnerability and Community is licensed under a Creative Commons Attribution-Share Alike 3.0 United States License, and can be copied without limit—including for commercial distribution—so long as it is attributed to Gary Chartier.

The cover image is *David danser foran arken* (2010), by Calvin. This work is licensed under the Creative Commons Attribution-Share Alike 3.0 Unported license. You are free to share (to copy, distribute and transmit the work) and to remix (to adapt the work), under the following conditions: attribution—you must attribute the work in the manner specified by the author or licensor (but not in any way that suggests that they endorse you or your use of the work); and share alike—if you alter, transform, or build upon this work, you may distribute the resulting work only under the same license as this one or a relevantly similar license.

The photograph of the author is *Gary Chartier SFL*, by Judd Weiss. It is licensed under the Creative Commons Attribution-Share Alike 2.0 Generic license. You are free to copy, distribute and transmit each image and to adapt it—provided that you attribute the image in the manner specified (but not in any way that suggests that the photographer endorses you or your use of the work) and that, if you alter, transform, or build upon this work, you may distribute the resulting work only under the same license as this one or a relevantly similar license.

This book was printed in the United States of America on acid-free paper.

This corrected printing is the second printing of this book.

ISBN 978-0-692-49412-7

Gary Chartier.
Vulnerability and Community: Meditations on the Spiritual Life
1. Meditations 2. Sermons—American
3. Sermons—Seventh-day Adventist authors I. Title

For
Fritz Guy, Robert Dunn,
Kathleen Dunn, and Kenneth Sutter

Contents

Introduction 1

Part I—Faith and Tradition 3
   1. Security 4
   2. When Religion Becomes an Idol 8
   3. Believing without Seeing 13
   4. Having Faith 17
   5. A Living Organism 21
   6. How to Handle God 24

Part II—Conduct and Character 28
   7. Choose Life 29
   8. Keeping the Law 32
   9. The Ten Commandments and War in the Middle East.........36
  10. Faith and Faithlessness 40
  11. Farewell to Retribution 44
  12. Power and Violence 48
  13. The Exodus Legacy 52
  14. On Being Good Shepherds 56
  15. Kings 60
  16. Fishing for People..64
  17. Jesus Was a Jew 68

Part III—Identity and Community 71
  18. What Makes Us What We Are? 72
  19. A Community of Love 77
  20. Jesus at the Party 81
  21. Dancing to the Flute 85
  22. The Good News of Belonging...89
  23. Insiders and Outsiders 93
  24. An Invitation to the Feast 97
  25. On Being Prodigal 101
  26. A House for God..105

27. Mattering 108
28. Encouraging Community 112
29. All Nations Stream to the Mountain 116
30. Heaven on Earth 118
31. Hospitality to the Stranger..................................122
32. A New Humanity...126
33. The Still, Small Voice 129
34. Surprising Forms of Grace 133

Part IV—Providence and Vulnerability..............................137
35. Rejoicing without the Messiah? 138
36. The Opiate of the Masses 142
37. God in History...146
38. Dry Bones, New Life...150
39. Treasures Old and New..154
40. Have No Fear! 158
41. Yearning and Connection 162
42. "My God, My God, Why Have You Forsaken Me?" 166
43. The Foolishness of the Cross 170
44. What's Wrong with Wisdom? 175
45. Peace and Deliverance 179
46. The Crucified Donkey..182
47. On Being a Victim..186
48. Everybody Suffers 190
49. Binding Up the Body..194
50. The End of Sacrifice 197

Part V—Passion and Delight 201
51. "I Want Never Got" 202
52. Seven Years 206
53. The Dancing King 210
54. The Glory of God..214

About the Author 219

Introduction

These meditations convey what I hope will prove to be useful perspectives on the spiritual life in today's world. They often approach the same or similar themes and topics and sometimes the same biblical texts. They are relatively self-contained, free-standing. But they are united by two central emphases: *first*, an understanding of God as vulnerable to the choices of creatures—and thus as experiencing delight and suffering along with them—and a consequent awareness that remotely credible talk of God's activity in the world must understand it as at least almost always persuasive rather than coercive; and, *second*, a perception of flourishing religious communities as vulnerable, and so as inclusive. These emphases are interwoven throughout.

The meditations contained in Part I examine the nature of religion and religious belief. Those in Part II consider the implications of faith for what we do and who we are. Part III explores the nature of community, with a particular emphasis on the notion of a kind of community that finds its identity precisely in rejecting the insider-outsider distinction that is so central to the identities of so many communities—notably religious ones. The reflections in Part IV focus on the historical presence and activity of the God who is vulnerable, while those in Part V emphasize the worth of passionate delight in the vulnerable God's good creation.

My goal here is to present an attractive and realistic understanding of the spiritual life, as a life lived in the face of ambiguity but marked with the potential for enjoyment, growth, and responsible action. I am no master of this life, but I hope that what I have concluded will be helpful to those who read what I have written. Their own experiences will doubtless be different in important ways; may we all bring our own stories to bear on the task of living together in God's world.

I hope it is clear that I do not presume to anything like certainty regarding what I say in this book. Even when I seem to *assert*, I am speaking of what I hope and think I may be able to defend, not of knowledge I claim to possess, propositions I can confidently report, or insights I imagine myself to have grasped perfectly. These meditations involve the working-out of a possible vision, not the report of proofs or confident certainties or infallible disclosures. The very focus on vulnerability and contingency that is expressed in the meditations themselves underlies their creation and informs my attitude toward them.

I belive we should assume that God can communicate meaningfully in and through human words and ideas that, because they are human, reflect human finitude, fallibility, and sin—and that were not necessarily intended by those who spoke or wrote or heard by those who first read or listened as answering the questions *we* may find most pressing. I frequently bracket questions about the history that lies behind a given biblical story, focusing instead on the canonical form of the story (whether I say so explicitly or not). When I do, it's not because I think the historical questions are either settled or unimportant, but because this isn't a scholarly treatise (my book *The Analogy of Love* develops some of the relevant issues more fully) and because there are insights to be gleaned from biblical stories quite apart from the answers to these questions.

Fritz Guy, Ken Sutter, and A. Ligia Radoias, among others, have commented helpfully at various points on these meditations in draft, though each will surely disagree with various things I say here. The welcome influence of the late Marcus Borg on my characterization of the politics and culture of first-century Palestine and Jesus' role in relation to both should be thoroughly evident throughout, as should the inspiration—both literary and substantive—provided by such adepts at the form I essay here as Nicholas Lash, Austin Farrer, John Bowker, Marilyn McCord Adams, Brian Hebblethwaite, Rowan Williams, and David Brown. Brad Whited deserves thanks for encouraging me to pursue publication of what is now a portion of Chapter 2. And of course I happily acknowledge the usual suspects—Lalé Welsh, A. Ligia Radoias, Aena Prakash, Alexander Lian, Andrew Howe, Annette Bryson, Carole Pateman, Charles W. Teel, Jr., David B. Hoppe, David Gordon, David R. Larson, Deborah K. Dunn, Donna Carlson, Elenor Webb, Eva Pascal, Fritz Guy, Jeffrey Cassidy, Jesse Leamon, John Thomas, Maria Zlateva, Nabil Abu-Assal, Patricia M. Cabrera, Roger E. Rustad, Jr., Ronel Harvey, Sheldon Richman, W. Kent Rogers, Wonil Kim, and Xavier Alasdhair Kenneth Doran—for the usual reasons.

Part I
Faith and Tradition

1
Security

There are few things I want more than security—the feeling of strong, warm arms holding me tight; the sound of a reassuring voice whispering confidently that everything will be OK. There's something profoundly empowering and liberating about security.

We can sense the power that comes from feeling secure in the psalmist's meditation. "Jahweh is the stronghold of my life," he exults. "[O]f whom shall I be afraid?"

The word "covenant" is a rich word, a word that evokes in me a sense of undergirding and unconditional love. It suggests rock-solid security. Generations of faithful Jews must have felt deep assurance reading the words of Genesis 15. "No one but your very own issue shall be your heir," God is depicted as saying. And, even more: "To your descendants I give this land, from the river of Egypt to the great river, the river Euphrates."

Land matters. Realizing that there is *some place* that is *my place* is an especially moving experience of security. When I was in graduate school in England, I always looked forward to returning to California. Even when the LA basin was drenched in smog, touching down at LAX was exhilarating. Driving to Corona along the 91 freeway to the Pierce Street off ramp, turning left, and making my way toward La Sierra University was even more exhilarating. Having a place called home is crucial to stable personal identity. It offers meaning. It offers tangible roots.

One of the acids eating away at social solidarity in America is the restless rootlessness that afflicts so many people. Always on the move, always changing jobs, they find it harder to develop deep, close ties. We have become a nation of strangers. And one potential remedy is a sense of connection to places that offer us meaning and identity. It can be good news indeed if there is a place that is really mine, really *ours*.

Just because it is so strong, though, the desire for security can spur us to act unjustly and destructively. There is nothing wrong with wanting security. But because it is so valuable, it can become a temptation.

Consider Herod. Not prepared—according to the passion narratives—to kill Jesus outright, he was nonetheless disturbed by Jesus—puzzled and hostile. If Herod *did* plot to kill Jesus at some earlier time, as the Pharisees suggest in Luke 13, it would hardly be surprising. Jesus threatened Herod by calling into question his way of life and the social and political order he helped to maintain.

But the Jesus of Luke 15 doesn't let his interlocutors off the hook by focusing only on *Herod*'s opposition to God's project in the world. It is not only the foreign Herod, it is "Jerusalem, Jerusalem" which "kills the prophets and stones those who are sent to it." The drive toward security can turn into idolatry even in a community, like ours, that believes it has rejected the grip of idols.

That grip is evident *whenever* a community seeks to obliterate those who are different—those whose ideas or lifestyles challenge the dominant consensus and unsettle the confidence of those unwilling to consider alternatives to the prevailing way of life. Jesus' Jewish contemporaries may have reacted in horror when the Romans erected *statues* in their midst; but they, too, could idolize security—as Herod did, and as we do.

It is painfully ironic now to read Genesis 15 and the glorious hope it embodies of an Israel stretching from Egypt to the Euphrates. It is all too apparent today how readily a beautiful dream like this can easily become an idol. The entirely appropriate drive for a sense of place has prompted Abraham's descendants to kill and maim and vilify as they squabble over his legacy. When the memory of past injustice has grown so faint that yesterday's victims become today's oppressors, when violence becomes so casually accepted a tool of government policy that a botched assassination attempt can be criticized because it was botched, and not because it was an assassination attempt—then we can see how powerful the idolatry of *place*, of security, really is.

Paul reminds his readers that the ultimate source of their security is God. The psalmist is sure that God is his stronghold. Jesus appears serenely confident in the face of Herod's threat. This kind of confidence highlights for us what freedom from the idolatrous quest for *security at any price* really means.

It does *not* mean rejecting creation as valueless. After all, God has made and is making it. Nor does it mean ceasing to love deeply and passionately and vulnerably. That's just what God does. We need look no further than the Cross to see that God loves too much not to be vulnerable.

To be sure, the attempted rejection of idolatry has sometimes taken the form of a rejection of creation, as if creation and God were in competition for our attention. But that's not the point at all. Indeed, this sort of rejection can amount to a new kind of idolatry, an idolatry of the religious practices and institutions to which we flee from the rest of the created world. God and creation *can't* compete. If they could, they would be on the same level; they would be the same *kind* of reality. And so God wouldn't be God at all.

No: idolatry is treating some aspect, any aspect of creation as if it were ultimate, as if it were God. That's bad for whatever we idolize—no person or place can bear the infinite responsibility of offering us complete and absolute security. Too often, we seek to manipulate and control the persons, places, and institutions we idolize to *guarantee* that they will provide the security we seek. Idolatry is bad for the rest of creation—which we're likely to treat unjustly as we defend the inflated claims we believe our idols rightly exert. And it's bad for us: no creature can deliver ultimate fulfillment, so idolatry is bound to disappoint us.

Rejecting idolatry means accepting that we can rest confidently in God. It means knowing, with Paul, that our home is in heaven—not in the sense that we don't belong on this beautiful planet, but in the sense that God—who is, after all, here with us now, not hiding in some remote portion of the universe—is always and everywhere our true home.

God loves us and is present with and to and for us amidst all the circumstances of our valuable and important ordinary lives. Rejecting idolatry means, with David, living all the days of our lives in the home that God prepares for us, the home that God *is*. Being at home with God is not a matter of running away from God's good world into monastic isolation. It is living out of a deep-seated recognition of God's unconditional grace in a way that frees us from the oppression that is idolatry, that frees us to seek out as much security as the good creation can offer us while knowing that even when creation disappoints us, we are still embraced by God's love.

2
When Religion Becomes an Idol

Religion is powerful. It shapes behavior in profound ways. It can exert enormous influence on people's lives. So it is understandable that kings and priests and disciples would all seek to control it.

When Jeroboam establishes a new center of worship, his immediate purpose is to ensure the loyalty of his subjects—if they worship in Judah rather than Israel, they may ultimately decide to serve Judah's rather than Israel's king; consequently, he manufactures two golden calves, announcing that *these* are the gods who brought Israel out of Egypt. Jesus' opponents attempt to take his life because his authority is independent of their own. The Jerusalem establishment challenges his followers as well, questioning on what basis they have healed a blind beggar.

We all face the temptation to claim divine endorsement for our own religious beliefs and practices. Not even the disciples are immune. As we read the gospels, we discern their confusion and doubt. Tracing the history of the early church, we see again how divisive were their debates, how diverse their opinions. *And yet* encountering Jesus alive after his death, these disciples—the same ones who had been confused before, the same ones who would be confused again—declare with absolute confidence that God is unequivocally and unilaterally on their side. Note how they pray in Acts: everything that happens is ascribed to the purpose and power of God.

This kind of stance sounds pious, to be sure, but it really represents the arrogant claim that we enjoy a God's-eye view of the world, that *our perspectives* are identical with *God's truth*. When we identify our projects, our proclamations, with God's will, then we do not need to take responsibility for assessing them critically. We do not need to listen to those who disagree. What such an approach misses is that God's communication with us is colored, limited, conditioned, affected by what we are prepared to say and hear. Our understanding of truth is progressive. The reality is that all of us are more or less like Jeroboam: the gods we invite others to worship, the gods we worship ourselves, are pathetic images of our own construction. There is no language about God or God's activity in the world that is not the language of finite, fallible, and sinful creatures, no discourse about God that is not constrained by presuppositions and metaphors drawn from our own experience and ultimately inadequate to characterize our infinite creator. God is always greater than, and different from, the images we shape and express in our theology, our doctrine, our ethics, our worship, and our prayer.

Any finite reality that is allowed to trump the claims of all other realities, that is treated as infinite in value and authority, is an idol. Perfectly good things—loyalty to place, sensory pleasure, social service—can become false gods when they tyrannize our lives. We can *see* the falsity of many of our idols easily enough (though we often find it hard to *do* anything about them). But it is often harder to see that our religious language and belief and practice become idolatrous when we treat them as if they themselves were divine. When we identify cultural forms now dead or dying with what is permanently and absolutely good for life in society; when we accept as divine mandates obligations imposed on us by social convention; when we allow the real or imagined disapproval of a religious community to stifle us; when we equate ideas constructed using the vocabulary and assumptions of an earlier era with unchanging truth; when we permit ourselves to be inhibited by doubt or shame or guilt; when we allow theological or moral abstractions to get in the way of our quest for concrete truth and love, we are crafting fresh idols, no more worthy of worship than those Jeroboam erected in Bethel and Dan.

This does not mean, of course, that every idea we have inherited, every apparent truth we have discovered, should be rejected as simply wrong. To avoid idolizing the convictions we have inherited from our churches, families, friends, and other communities does not require that we reject all our beliefs out of hand as necessarily false. What it *does* mean is that we should recognize that the habits, practices, perspectives, concepts, and feelings bequeathed us by others or crafted by ourselves are fallible, subject to revision and change. Neither the voice of the church nor the voice of the family nor the voice of the media nor the voice of the theologians nor the voice of conscience—which is itself shaped by all these other voices—is the voice of God. Each voice is a limited, constrained, human voice, which deserves to be respected as such, but *only* as such. As we realize this, the illusion of necessity, the patina of sanctity and infallibility, drops away. What may once have seemed self-evident and beyond question now becomes subject to critical assessment.

Challenging idolized religious systems or ideas is a necessity if we want to be free from their domination. To be sure, this is a difficult business. It can lead to a sense of overwhelming vertigo or crushing guilt. We're used to our idols; they've been around so long that they seem indistinguishable from the God whose place they have usurped. But we cannot avoid tension and turmoil if we are to find freedom from enslavement to the false gods that limit and constrict us and drive us apart from others.

One of my favorite stories tells us clearly, I think, what confronting a religious idol is like and why doing so matters so much. It is perhaps a bit long in the telling, but I think it is one we need to hear. Mark Twain's Huckleberry Finn and the escaped slave, Jim, are rafting along the Mississippi. Slowly, it begins to dawn on Huck that he's helping Jim find freedom from slavery:

> Jim said it made him all over trembly and feverish to be so close to freedom. Well, I can tell you it made me all over trembly and feverish, too, to hear him, because I begun to get it through my head that he was most free—and who was to blame for it? Why, me. I couldn't get that out of my conscience, no how nor no way. . . . I tried to make out to myself that I warn't to blame . . . ; but it warn't no use, conscience up and says, every time, "But you knowed he was running for his freedom, and you could 'a' paddled ashore and told somebody." . . . That was where it pinched. Conscience says to me, "What had poor Miss Watson done to you that you could see her . . . [slave] go off right under your eyes and never say one single word? What did that poor old woman do to you that you could treat her so mean?" . . . [And h]ere was this . . . [slave], which I had as good as helped to run away, coming right out flat-footed and saying he would steal his children [my ital.]—children that belonged to a man I didn't even know; a man that hadn't ever done me no harm. . . . My conscience got to stirring me up hotter than ever, until at last I says to it, "Let up on me—it ain't too late yet—I'll paddle ashore

at the first light and tell." I felt easy and happy and light as a feather right off. . . .

After Jim tells him he's the best friend he's ever had, and the only white man who's ever kept a promise to him, Huck begins to have second thoughts. "Well, I just felt sick," he tells us. "But I says, I *got* to do it—I can't get *out* of it." Nonetheless, Huck lies to keep some men from investigating the raft. Still feeling guilty, he resigns himself to his fate as a moral failure. But when Jim is captured, Huck again considers writing Jim's owner and telling her the location of her slave.

> The more I studied about this the more my conscience went to grinding me, and the more wicked and low-down and ornery I got to feeling. And at last, when it hit me all of a sudden that here was the plain hand of Providence slapping me in the face and letting me know my wickedness was being watched all the time from up there in heaven, . . . and now was showing me there's One that's always on the lookout, and ain't a-going to allow no such miserable doings to go only just so fur and no further, I most dropped in my tracks I was so scared. Well, I tried the best I could to kinder soften it up somehow for myself by saying I was brung up wicked, and so I warn't so much to blame; but something inside of my kept saying, "There was the Sunday School, you could 'a' gone to it; and if you'd 'a' done it they'd 'a' learnt you there that people that acts as I'd been acting about that . . . [slave] goes to everlasting fire."
>
> It made me shiver. And I about made up my mind to pray, and see if I couldn't try to quit being the kind of a boy I was and be better. So I kneeled down. But the words wouldn't come. Why wouldn't they? It warn't no use to try and hide it from Him. Nor from *me*, neither. I knowed very well why they wouldn't come. It was because my heart warn't right; it was because I warn't square; it was because I was playing double. I was letting *on* to give up sin, but away in side of me I was holding on to the biggest one of all. I was trying to make my mouth *say* I would do the right thing and the clean thing, and go and write to that . . . [slave's] owner and tell where he was; but deep down in me I knowed it was a lie, and He knowed it. You can't pray a lie—I found that out.

So Huck *does* write a letter to Jim's owner, telling her that Jim has been captured and where he can be found. For a moment, he feels spiritually refreshed. "I felt good and all washed clean of sin for the first time I had ever felt so in my life, and I knowed I could pray now. But I didn't do it straight off, but laid the paper down and set there thinking—thinking how good it was all this happened so, and how near I come to being lost and going to hell." But then, he says,

> ... somehow I couldn't seem to strike no places to harden me against ... [Jim], but only the other kind. I'd see him standing my watch on top of his'n, 'stead of calling me, so I could go on sleeping; and see him how glad he was when I come back out of the fog; and when I come to him again in the swamp ... ; and ... would always ... do everything he could think of for me, and how good he always was; ... and said I was the best friend old Jim ever had in the world, and the *only* one he's got now; and then I happened to look around and see that paper. ... I took it up, and held it in my hand. I was a-trembling, because I'd got to decide, forever, betwixt two things, and I knowed it. I studied a minute, sort of holding my breath, and then says to myself:
> "All right, then, I'll *go* to hell"—and tore it up.

Huck Finn was torn by the conflicting claims of different values: respect for a social order he believed had been ordained by God and love for his friend. He did not, of course, *really* reject God by rejecting this social order. But we can understand, given what he had been taught, why he thought he had done so. We can never be sure in such cases; there may not be a single right answer to a moral dilemma we face—there may be many acceptable responses. And even if there is only one, we are unlikely to perceive it with blinding clarity. Facing off against the idols is thus always a risky business.

Huck had no choice but to throw off the shackles of guilt in order to love. Challenging the idol that was his conscience, the idol that was the accumulated weight of tradition and convention that told him slavery was God's will, was the only way to achieve liberation—for himself and for Jim. He disregarded much of what he thought he knew was right for the sake of a love that called him to smash the idols that imprisoned him. The process was painful for him, and it will be for us. But it is one in which we must engage if we are to avoid the worship of human, all-too-human, golden calves at our own Bethels and Dans.

3
Believing without Seeing

It makes sense to doubt, as the Fourth Gospel describes Thomas as doing, if you think about it. Like their twenty-first-century counterparts, people in the first century didn't think it very likely that bodies vanished from tombs or that people known to be dead engaged their friends in conversation.

So Thomas's behavior is quite understandable and thoroughly reasonable. But—the story in the Fourth Gospel has it—he is mistaken. It's not, however, until he personally encounters Jesus that he acknowledges the truth of what his friends have told him: Jesus is truly alive.

The Fourth Gospel is a complex, sophisticated text, with multiple purposes and layers of meaning. But I think it's fair to say that *one* important function of the Thomas story, at least, is to provide an occasion for Jesus to say what he does at last to Thomas: "Have you believed because you have seen me? Blessed are those who have not seen and yet have come to believe?"

"Those who have not seen and yet have come to believe" are, of course, almost all of the Gospel's readers and hearers, including us. Thomas and his friends may have come to believe because of personal experience—*seeing*—that, despite his crucifixion and death, Jesus was truly alive. But, the evangelist seems to want to say, that doesn't make them members of a spiritually elite cadre of believers. Those who believe because of *testimony*, those who have not seen but have only heard, are truly blessed. They're not second-class Christians. There's no spiritual gap between the first witnesses and the rest of us.

We're still tempted to discount beliefs based on the testimony of others or handed on to us by our communities in favor of those grounded in our own experience. We'd like to believe that *our* vision, *our* insight, are responsible for our beliefs. We'd like to think they were *our* products, *our* creations. One of the things we *learn*, ironically enough, from *our culture* is that we must supposedly justify all of our beliefs with reference to basic truths that no rational person could reasonably reject, or at least come up on our own with adequate evidence to entail them. We're taught to doubt our beliefs until they have been justified in this way. Beliefs handed on to us by others, through tradition or testimony, are at best second-class.

But the Fourth Gospel prompts us to ask whether this is truly appropriate, whether it really makes sense. None of us begins to think about her or his beliefs from a neutral vantage point; each of us begins somewhere. And that seems perfectly reasonable, on reflection. When we think about our beliefs, we can appropriately start "in the middle," with the beliefs we have, beliefs derived from our traditions and communities.

To use an analogy made famous by the philosopher Otto Neurath, we're like sailors at sea: we can rebuild our boat at best plank by plank. Unless we want to drown, however, we can't remove the hull and start reconstructing our entire ship over all at once. At any given time, most of the planks with which we're working will be the ones already in place. The same is true of our beliefs. We rightly reflect on them, criticizing and reworking them and making them our own. But it would be absurd to abandon them all and try to begin in a vacuum to determine what to believe. We are within our rights to believe what we already do, in fact, believe—what, for instance, we have acquired from tradition or testimony—unless we know of good reasons not to do so.

While I don't need to go masochistically in search of reasons to doubt my convictions, if I become aware of a reasonable challenge to one of my beliefs, I will need to come to terms with this challenge—by determining that I need not be troubled by the challenge or by altering the challenged belief or some other belief. I can't rest content with what I've inherited no matter what challenges I confront. But I do not have to find arguments which prove my beliefs in advance before I am free to endorse the convictions I actually have. Whatever the origins of our beliefs, we do not have to wait for conclusive arguments in their support before we can accept them legitimately.

Thus, for instance, if we believe that Jesus' disciples encountered him in person after his death, we must be aware of and responsive to reasonable objections to this belief. But if these objections can be met responsibly, we need not wait, with Thomas, for incontrovertible positive evidence before acknowledging Jesus as alive. We need not suspend a belief we already have until we've amassed indubitable evidence in its favor.

It makes sense to start with the beliefs I have not only because they *are* the beliefs I have, but also because they have been winnowed by time. As Stephen Clark observes:

> The refusal to accept another's word or take for one's basis a theory one cannot oneself demonstrate can only be supposed to be our duty by someone who has quite forgotten what she herself is bound to do in every area of life. We live within a sea of testimony: everything that we ordinarily count upon has been handed on to us; the very possibility of demonstrating anything itself rests on our having been initiated into the techniques and presuppositions of the testifying community. . . .
>
> We can legitimately conclude that not all well-established beliefs are true, and that we must leave ourselves some room for manœuvre not to be tied down to one doctrine merely because people in the past have thought it true. But it does not follow that long-established beliefs and practices have no greater claim on our practical and theoretical allegiance than newly minted ones. They have the signal advantage that they are there, that their ramifications have, to some extent, been explored, that we have some idea of what they really amount to. Old doctrines are not true merely because they are old, any more than new ones are true because they are new: but it is not absurd to suggest that the old ones have our prior allegiance, that they do not need to establish themselves on just the same terms as new theories, that they have, as it were, the benefit of the doubt.

There is no shame, then, in believing without seeing, in believing because of "say so," because of tradition and testimony. There is no shame in admitting that we are part of an ongoing tradition in which we depend on innumerable past generations for insight and understanding. Each new generation must, of course, rethink and revise what it has inherited from the past. No healthy tradition is static. But we may nonetheless begin where we are, accepting what we have been given as a reasonable starting point for our own reflection, analysis, construction, synthesis, and speculation.

Like the believers for whom the Fourth Gospel was written, we can acknowledge that we are not the masters of our own beliefs, that we rely on others as others, in turn, will rely on us. We can affirm that we understand God's way with us and with the world, not alone but *together*, in company with numberless others past and future.

4
Having Faith

The word "faith" carries so many different meanings. It can mean *reliance on authority as a means of insight into God's nature and purposes*. Mediæval Christians were often encouraged to accept "on faith" the pronouncements of church authorities about doctrinal issues. It can serve as a synonym for *ungrounded, immediate intuition*, as when someone says, "I just have faith that God is real." It can mean, as for the Reformers, *the trustful acceptance of God's forgiveness*. It can simply serve as a synonym for *religious belief*, as when we talk about, say, "what Christian faith means today." The meanings are strikingly different. The only thing that unites them seems to be a denial of autonomy, an acknowledgment that one can't manage on one's own.

In Hebrews 11, *faith* seems to refer to *confidence in God's steadfastness*. What God has promised, God will do. And the writer to the Hebrews may have been especially concerned with God's willingness to fulfill what the writer believed were specific, verbal promises. So those of us who are unsure that divine commitments come wafting down out of heaven off of God's LaserWriter may wonder if the praise of faith in Hebrews is really relevant to us. We don't receive specific assurances of this kind, and we don't know anyone else who has, either. But the opening words of the "faith chapter" point to an understanding of faith that can persist, I think, even if God's good will toward us isn't expressed in promises like those we make each other, and even if God's self-revelation isn't expressed in unambiguous verbal formulations.

Faith, says Hebrews 11, "is the assurance of things hoped for, the conviction of things not seen." Faith, then, is what allows us to hang on when things aren't clear and distinct. Faith is ultimately about being grounded, about living with a sense that one's life has meaning and value and purpose. It is the confidence that one is at home in the universe, not an alien—that the universe is at root a friendly place.

It's not that specific religious beliefs or practices are irrelevant to faith in this sense. The shape faith takes, the understanding of faith we endorse, the justification for faith we advance—all will vary with our beliefs. But faith itself is not cognitive, even if it has cognitive implications and presuppositions; it is a fundamental stance or orientation of the self, a matter of what psychologists, philosophers, and theologians call *basic trust*.

It is important not to confuse faith in this sense with naïve optimism. Having faith doesn't mean pretending that one has knowledge when one doesn't, assuming that one can see clearly when one can't. If everything were clear, there would be no need to talk about "the conviction of things *not seen*." All of those to whom Hebrews 11 refers navigated through obscurity and darkness, unsure what to expect even as they relied on God. As they are described in this moving chapter, they may sometimes have had more confidence in particular, specifiable outcomes than we may regard as realistic. But they suffered from no illusions about their ability to comprehend or manage the future. Faith is not a way of asserting control over the future; it is a way of living when we lack such control—which is to say, *always*.

That's a point worth bearing in mind as we read Luke 12. "Do not be afraid, little flock," Jesus tells his audience, "for it is your Father's good pleasure to give you the kingdom." The Third Evanglist depicts Jesus as envisioning himself and those to whom he speaks as caught up in a dramatic movement toward God's future. Something exciting and new is happening—and is about to happen—in and through his ministry. Despite the uncertainty and danger accompanying this change, those who listen to Jesus can be confident. They need not fear. And because they need not fear, they need not cling to their possessions as a source of security in the face of impending distress: they can give generously to those in need. At the same time, this confidence does not tell them just what is going to happen, or when. "[I]f the owner of the house had known at what hour the thief was coming, he would not have let his house be broken into."

The assumption that we have everything nailed down—that we know all the truth, that we can secure on our own the meaning and value of our own lives—is something that, ironically, is all-too-often confused with faith. In fact, it is the opposite of faith, the foundation of all those self-destructive and other-destructive attempts at self-securing that contribute so much misery to our world. This kind of self-securing often takes a religious guise. Notice Isaiah's condemnation of his contemporaries. Their offerings and religious gatherings are valueless. They seem to rely on these religious activities to assure them of their spiritual security. At the same time, however, they condone violence, injustice, and oppression.

It is not, of course, that there is anything wrong with religious observances. The psalmist affirms that those who are *thankful* offer the kind of sacrifice God wants. Explicit acknowledgment of God and God's activity in the world enables us to understand God, ourselves, and our world more fully and to align ourselves with what God is up to in the world. God does not eat the flesh of bulls or drink the blood of goats, the psalmist affirms in verse 13—and those of us with doubts about the wanton killing of our fellow creatures will agree. But God welcomes an attitude of thanksgiving.

Thanksgiving is of the essence of faith. To be thankful is to be receptive, to acknowledge the fact that what we have is a gift, not something we control and manage and own. In faith, we are rooted in what is not ourselves: it's not just that we are secure, but that we are *secured*, that we are not self-sustaining.

We see hints of faith in our lives and the lives of others all the time. Suppose someone does the right thing even when something else would be easier. Suppose someone acknowledges the gap between God's truth and her own perceptions. Suppose someone lets go of the desire to control a lover and offers her or him a frightening freedom, without retreating into a loveless world free of risk or vulnerability. Suppose someone refuses the false security of imagining that his own ideas are infallible—without lapsing into the skeptical doubt that no idea is better than any other. Here, we catch glimpses of the meaning of faith today.

Faith is about risk, then. It's about living in the tension-filled space between skepticism and optimism, between resignation and control. It is the only way one can live, though, once one acknowledges that one cannot grit one's teeth and guarantee how history will come out or what one's life will mean. It is the only way one can live in this kind of world—a world in which God's purposes are all-too-often often not realized, and in which God, too, can be surprised by the choices of creatures.

The Gospel story serves to give content to the conviction that faith is an appropriate response to the way things are. It does no offer knockdown, drag-out proofs. It is not coercive. But the story of Jesus provides us with a clue we can use to begin discerning the pattern of the whole, a pattern in which the universe is a friendly place, a pattern in which, despite all appearances, it makes sense to say, "Do not be afraid, little flock."

5
A Living Organism

The Christian church is a living organism. It is not defined by absolutely unchanging continuity of belief and practice, which have varied, in fact, quite dramatically over time. It is an ongoing conversation, linked by a common memory with the dramatic events of Jesus ministry, crucifixion, and life beyond death.

Memory is on center-stage as Peter reflects, in Acts, on the need for a new apostle who will replace Judas. "It is necessary," he says, "to choose one of the men who have been with us the whole time the Lord Jesus went in and out among us, beginning from John's baptism to the time when Jesus was taken up from us. For one of these must become a witness with us of his resurrection." To qualify as an apostle, one must be able to keep the memory of Jesus alive, to testify to what he was and what he meant.

First John observes: "we accept man's testimony, but God's testimony is greater." But God's testimony, what God says to us, is always, unavoidably, mediated to us through the testimony of other people. Divine revelation does not reach us on a print-out straight from God's LaserWriter. Rather, people experience, they remember, and they tell. We all, of necessity, believe on say-so. And, despite the reference to "God's testimony" in apparent contrast to human testimony, 1 John recognizes just this: "I write these things to you who believe in the name of the Son of God so that you may know that you have eternal life." *I write*—the author bears witness to God's grace, offering insight and reassurance.

The importance of *tradition*, of *testimony*, of *passing on*, are on center stage in John 17. "I have revealed you to those whom you gave me out of the world. They were yours; you gave them to me and they have obeyed your word. Now they know that everything you have given me comes from you. For I gave them the words you gave me and they accepted them. . . . I have given them your word." Again, there is the sense of truth being handed on—first to Jesus, and then to the apostles.

One the one hand, we cannot avoid believing on say-so. At first, we learn everything we learn from mothers and fathers and teachers and friends. And even as educated adults, we must still take a great deal on the word of others: we depend on experts in fields from accounting to history to physiology to physics. And we can rightly rely on ideas that have been tested in the proving-ground of tradition. Most of us don't pretend to start from scratch and think through the options neutrally until we arrive at rationally compelling beliefs. But we may feel vaguely irresponsible intellectually because we haven't, and we sometimes imagine that our beliefs are legitimate only if we can prove that we could have arrived at them in this way.

One need not start from narrow, limited premises and try to reconstruct one's beliefs about God any more than one can do so with one's beliefs about the external world, other people, and so forth. One can challenge and rebut and modify these beliefs. But one begins with the beliefs one has, most of which are derived from one's traditions and communities. When we think about our beliefs, we can appropriately start "in the middle." We can begin by trusting those who have taught us, accepting the beliefs we actually have, even though we need to be alert to potential challenges.

Of course, we may well end up accepting what Psalm 1 calls "the counsel of the wicked" if we accept beliefs on say-so *uncritically*. We have to be sensitive to potential inconsistencies in our traditions. We have to listen thoughtfully to challenges—and not to assume that, just because someone challenges our beliefs, she or he therefore qualifies as "wicked" or "scornful." Instead, we have to ask carefully, thoughtfully, reflectively how to integrate what we learn as we confront our own doubts and the challenges of others into what has been handed onto us—into our tradition.

The thing to remember is that this is precisely what tradition *is*. We begin somewhere in particular. We trust the testimony and honor the insight of those whose work and prayer are the font from which Christianity has emerged. But we recognize that the handing-on process continues—and that we are part of it. To recognize the value of testimony, the worth of say-so, is to acknowledge that we, too, have a part to play in passing on our tradition. God's work in and through the church cannot be imagined to have ended with the death of the last person who remembered Jesus personally. The process of testifying continues—and we're part of it.

Unavoidably, we lack the direct experience of the candidates considered by the apostles in Acts 1, or the capacity to testify directly to which the author of 1 John appeals. Indeed, we may feel as if our own role as those who help to continue the tradition, to continue the conversation, is as random as that of Matthias, remembered as having been picked by lot to replace Judas. But, even as we respect and learn from centuries of tradition, we must simultaneously be willing and ready to participate in the ongoing process of helping that tradition to grow, bringing our own experience and reasoning and reflection and insight—limited as they are—to the task. The Christian tradition grows because of *us*. And God can work through us, just as God could work through an apostle selected at random, to keep it growing and alive.

6
How to Handle God

I find parts of 1 John poetically, almost painfully, beautiful. To hear the words of the epistle's first chapter is, for me, to be transported to another world. It is a world of early morning stillness and ritual celebration, a world of high-vaulted cathedral ceilings off which echo the angelically pure voices of preadolescent choristers, a world marked by things I associate reflexively with transcendence. The words are powerful. I think I can understand why the college boyfriend of a friend offered her a translation of 1 John from Greek into English as a gift.

But even as I am touched by the beauty of 1 John, I also have to acknowledge something that troubles me about it. Note how it begins: the readers are assured that what they are being told depends on "what we have heard, what we have seen with our eyes, what we have looked at and touched with our hands, concerning the word of life." They are told that "this life was revealed, and we have seen it and testify to it, and declare to you the eternal life that was with the Father and was revealed to us."

The kind of experience in view here differs radically from mine—and, I suspect, from yours as well. For *we* have not heard or seen or touched Jesus of Nazareth. Does authentic spirituality depend on our having done so? Asking questions of this sort makes it easy to feel inferior, to wonder whether one's spiritual life is good enough, whether it is authentic at all.

Austin Farrer had this sort of problem. The sense that a vital religious experience, an authentic one, involved a dramatic confrontation with God of a kind that was unmistakably evident caused him considerable dis-ease as an adolescent. He writes:

> I thought of myself as set over against deity as one man faces another across a table, except that God was invisible and indefinitely great. And I hoped that he would signify his presence to me by way of colloquy;

but neither out of the scripture I read nor in the prayers I tried to make did any mental voice address me. I believe at that time anything would have satisfied me, but nothing came: no 'other' stood beside me, no shadow of presence fell upon me.

And it was not until he began to rethink how God is present and active in the world that he found liberation from his doubts:

> I would no longer attempt, with the psalmist, 'to set God before my face'. I would see him as the underlying cause of my thinking, especially of those thoughts in which I tried to think of him. I would dare to hope that sometimes my thought would become diaphanous, so that there should be some perception of the divine cause shining through the created effect, as a deep pool, settling into a clear tranquility, permits us to see the spring in the bottom of it from which its waters rise. . . .
>
> [B]y so viewing my attempted work of prayer, I was rid of the frustration which had baffled me before. And this is why, when Germans set their eyeballs and pronounce the terrific words 'He speaks to thee' (Er redet dich an) I am sure, indeed, that they are saying something, but I am still more sure that they are not speaking to my condition.

How did Farrer learn to read his experience as mediating God's presence? Because he was *taught* to do so within the Christian community, because he was immersed in a tradition that provided him with a way of understanding what happened to him. As we learn to see our experience through Christian eyes, we come to experience Gods activity throughout our lives. Our experience acquires meaning within the context provided by the collection of beliefs, practices, images, and ways of talking that we are taught as Christians. It is as we critically appropriate the "traditioning" offered us by the Christian community that we come to understand and interpret our experience Christianly. Christian belief does not depend on our having had experiences of God's presence like those Farrer was looking for, or those to which 1 John 1 alludes.

Perhaps one way to read the story of Thomas in John 20 is to see it as designed to counteract this sort of fear. While Thomas has seen the risen Christ and believed on the basis of his own experience, others who will hear the testimony of the Apostles may also enjoy rich intimacy with God. The Apostles' experience does not confer privileged status upon them. God is always available. And we can come into contact with divine grace and power as we learn the Christian story, a story handed down to us by a living community of faith rooted in the experience of those like the early Christians who speak to us through 1 John.

We come to read our experience aright as we learn to live in the community of faith. Living in this community immerses us in the Christian story, helps us to identify with it make it our own. But community is not only the vehicle by which we learn the story; it is itself an integral *part* of the story.

Learning to be a Christian means learning to own oneself as a part of God's *good* creation. This means, on the one hand, accepting one's life as God's good gift; thus, it means celebrating with joy the richness of relationships. It means accepting that we are given life and identity and meaning in part through those who love us—and thus that we are not God, that we do not make ourselves, that we do not dwell in self-sufficient, Olympian splendor. And so, in turn, it means embracing their love with giddy delight, acknowledging their love as "precious oil on the head, running down upon the beard, on the beard of Aaron, running down over the collar of his robes."

Learning to be a Christian also means learning to own oneself as a *part* of God's good creation, as finite, as anything but the center of reality. It means recognizing the myriad ways in which one is limited by the reality of others, claimed by their need, challenged by their otherness. When we begin to love otherness, when we respond in love to the needs of others as did the Jerusalem church, we have made a profoundly important step in the direction of letting God be God. For God can be encountered aright only when I cease to idolize myself or to enslave myself in idolatry to any other finite reality.

Christians proclaim the risen Christ because they have learned to read their experience in particular ways, not because they have undergone paranormal visitations of one sort or another. In the school of Christian discipleship, they have been taught the Christian story. On the basis of this story, they identify God using the story of Jesus even as they recognize God's presence and activity everywhere.

Christians—and all other people—encounter God in all times and places. But we respond aright to the One thus encountered as we learn to let God be God. We do so in part as we learn to love otherness in the community of the church, and the other communities—cities, friendships, families—to which we belong. On the one hand, we accept that we are not God because our lives are gifts, gifts given in part in and through the love of others. And we also let God be God as we accept the *reality* of others and their consequent claims on us.

Obscurity surrounds us. But there is Light in the world, too. In community, we learn the story that frees us from the hold of darkness. And as we respond aright to the joys and challenges of community, we move toward the light. In the beginning was love. Divine love prompts the sharing of the story out of which we live; divine love prompts us to receive it; and divine love prompts us, in turn, to love in ways that enable us to own ourselves as parts of God's good creation, so that we may come ever more clearly to see the One who is light, in whom is no darkness at all.

Part II
Conduct and Character

7
Choose Life

Obey and live; disobey and die. The contrast in Deuteronomy is stark and clear. On first reading, it is easy to see in this statement of alternatives an appeal, not to reason or to love, but to fear. To secure conformity, God threatens the recalcitrant with annihilation.

This may be how the original readers understood it. But, if so, as we seek to heed its inspiring call to "choose life," perhaps we can conceive of the relationship among divine action, moral behavior, and death differently than they did.

A popular account of the relationship between God and morality suggests that the moral quality of our behavior and our characters reflects God's arbitrary assignment of value to some actions and states of affairs and disvalue to others. On this view, what is wrong with murder or adultery is that they make God angry, and what is right about love is that it makes God happy. (Proponents of this view fail to explain *why* these things make God angry, and why whatever it is that makes God angry isn't enough to explain why we should avoid them.) God could perfectly well decide tomorrow that cruelty was the order of the day.

In fact, however—let me assert here without arguing—what is moral is what is good for creation, what makes for the flourishing of sentient creatures. What is good for creation is what is appropriate to the way in which it has been formed by God's creative work. And the shape of that creative work is, in turn, a reflection of God's own identity as ceaselessly outpoured love.

But if this is so, then the meaning Deuteronomy 30 can have for us here and now becomes clearer. Choosing life, choosing goodness, and choosing God are not three different things; at root, they are identical. To choose goodness is to choose God. To choose God is to choose life. To choose life is to choose goodness. To be sure, we may choose to oppress or ignore others to assert ourselves. But to do so is ultimately to choose against reality. It is to pretend to be God, and thus to cut oneself off from others. It is a mammoth exercise in self-deception.

Perhaps the same point is evident in Paul's challenge to the Corinthian Christians. When Paul talks about "the flesh," he doesn't mean the body, not the material, not the sensuous, but rather life in the sphere of sin. And to what does he point as evidence of fleshly life among the Corinthians but "jealousy and quarreling," which he suggests are sufficient conditions for their residence in the old æon from which he believed them to have been delivered by Christ.

Division is a sign of life according to the flesh because to opt for petty conflict is to opt for death. Jealousy and quarreling wound our spirits and sap our vitality. It's almost as if the jealous or violent person wills, if only in a small way, the death of the other. But in willing another's death, one also wills one's own. One wills one's own death because one chooses against the humanity one shares with her or him. One wills one's own death because one fractures oneself as a loving moral agent—willing the death of one's moral self. And one wills one's own death because one denies one's interdependence, one's embeddedness in the fabric of humanity. One chooses, again, to be God. Here again it must be emphasized that it is not that disobedience *leads* to death as the punishment imposed by an arbitrary God, but that every immoral act or trait is a dimension of the process of movement toward death. All sin is ultimately a kind of suicide.

All this may help us more clearly to understand the injunctions contained in the First Gospel's "Sermon on the Mount." Every moral choice forms the self—either in conformation to or in denial of reality. Interior acts as well as exterior ones shape the identity of the moral agent. And the subtle as well as the overt choice can promote or hinder the good of the other.

Thus, hatred fractures the self and undermines relation even when it does not issue in anger. In the same way, the spouse who immerses her- or himself in work may choose debilitating disunion whose effects are essentially the same as those of an emotional or sexual affair.

The person who takes a conventional oath unilaterally invokes God's support for personal, and perhaps idiosyncratic, plans and projects. And with what justification? Such a person, too, denies reality by treating her or his own agenda as divinely endorsed. The next best thing to *being* God is being able to guarantee that God will underwrite one's own position. But seeking to co-opt God is, again, to pretend that God isn't God at all. It is to presume to a level of authority or knowledge one does not and could not enjoy.

This is not the place to say all that needs saying about the First Gospel's pronouncement regarding divorce. Many would-be marital unions may be monuments to irrelation. Many may be vitiated by fraud. Many may not be grounded in unconditional commitments. But to shatter a genuine marriage, a relationship rooted in a commitment to unconditional love, in principle the embodiment of the most intimate kind of relation, to opt for disunion, is to do spiritual violence and to assail one's connectedness, one's embeddedness in relation. It is to choose something not unlike death for another, and so—directly and indirectly—for oneself.

Choosing life is not a straightforward business. As the famous prayer of Francis of Assisi reminds us, it is rather a paradoxical one. We live, not by hoarding life, but giving it in love. That is a conviction whose truth sometimes seems shrouded in darkness, as violence and disunion seem to dominate the human story. But our experience contains glimmers of insight, hints that the only kind of life worth living is the kind of life that values the good, that values love, more than mere living. We may find ourselves exclaiming with imprisoned psychiatrist Victor Frankl that love is what ultimately matters, what ultimately renders existence worthwhile. And those of us who have been captured by the Christian story may find in the doing and dying of Jesus the interpretive key to our experience that highlights the centrality of love as the way to choose life. That story emphasizes again that such choosing is not necessarily easy—that it may lead to what first seems like death. But it also declares, with a hope tempered by the agony of loss and abandonment on Calvary, that choosing as Jesus did may be precisely the way in which we must sometimes choose life, real life, the kind of life that matters.

8
Keeping the Law

Talk of keeping the law can sound oppressive. Law can be used as a club with which to beat outsiders and vulnerable people, those who don't fit in. And many laws lack genuine legitimacy. While the Declaration of Independence, for instance, may be read as implying that laws are justly enforceable in virtue of "the consent of the governed," this consent is persistently lacking. So-called "law enforcement" efforts lead to the imprisonment of millions of people in connection with the failed "war on drugs." Government officials who imprison others for violating their arbitrary edicts walk proudly free when they themselves disregard the laws they enforce on their subjects. But perhaps it is at moments like this when law is most important—not the laws enacted by creatures but the law of God, which is to say, the natural law.

Obviously, there's a difference between natural or divine law and human law, just as there's a difference between the sense in which God is personal and the sense in which we are persons. To talk about God's law is to speak in the language of analogy, of metaphor. Most fundamentally, human laws are acts of *will*. They're *chosen*. They could be other than they are. But we can't think of moral or natural law this way.

What we sometimes—let's remember that here, too, we're speaking metaphorically—refer to as *physical laws* or *the laws of nature* are contingent. They could just as well be other than they are. There's no metaphysical necessity about the fact that, say, the acceleration due to gravity on the earth's surface is 9.8 meters per second per second. The fact that we've got the particular laws of nature we do, laws that make our own existence possible as few others would is, indeed, among the most striking pointers to the reality of God. But we can't reasonably see what we sometimes call the *moral law* in the same way. The temperature at which water boils is, in a sense, arbitrary; the rightness or wrongness of, say, torture is not. To put the point succinctly: the truth or falsity of a moral judgment isn't a matter of divine *choice* any more than that of a logical or mathematical judgment is. It is simply the case that the volume of a cube can be determined by multiplying the lengths of its sides; in the same way, though moral truths aren't tautologies, it is simply the case that intentionally killing another person is wrong. It is no derogation from God's dignity or power to say that divine power cannot change moral any more than mathematical truths. Thus, we can reasonably refer to divine law as *natural* law.

One way of putting this is to say that morality is inextricably rooted in creation. Consider Psalm 19. We can start with verse 7: "The law of the LORD is perfect, reviving the soul." But it is important to note what has gone before, in the previous six verses. Here, the psalmist emphasizes the orderly, wondrous character of creation, beginning with the famous words, "The heavens declare the glory of God." It might appear that the two sections of the psalm are disconnected, but I think we would do well to see them as intimately linked. For the psalmist, the link probably consisted primarily in the fact that the order of nature and the moral law both reflected divine wisdom. We can continue to see the link this way if we understand that, while wisdom can discern many ways in which the created world might declare God's glory, divine wisdom will see that moral truth, like mathematical truth, is what it is because God's *creation* is what it is. What will count as flourishing, health, well-being for creation isn't something God could decide arbitrarily any more than the manufacturer of a car could decide arbitrarily what it might mean for the car to operate effectively. Because God has made *this* kind of world, what is good for what God has made follows naturally.

This means that we have every reason to attend to our own insights into what makes for happiness, well being, flourishing as we seek to discern what is right. So if someone claims that God endorses some putative requirement that doesn't protect creation from harm, or that actually *undermines* creation's flourishing, the simplest response will surely be that the person who claims this has just misunderstood God.

What the Hebrews came to call God's *wisdom* Greeks often identified as God's *Logos*. For both, the focus was on that in God which constitutes the order and meaning of the world. To say it is the divine wisdom or *Logos* or reason that constitutes the *moral* order in particular is not to say that what seems wise to us, the *conventional wisdom*, reveals what is morally right. As Paul reminds us in 1 Corinthians, God's wisdom and the conventional wisdom may be quite at odds. Today's conventional wisdom in too many places around the globe, for instance, is that preemptive war is inevitable, unavoidable, even if it is also unjust. Still, while—in the story of Jesus and elsewhere—we may see the flaws in the conventional wisdom, this is in the interests of disclosing what is morally appropriate in light of the way creation really is, not of introducing us to arbitrary divine edicts. We must be careful indeed that when we talk about divine law, we don't confuse God with the last of the mediæval emperors.

But this does not mean that using the metaphor of *law* to talk about moral norms has no meaning or value.

The language of law highlights the *objective* character of moral claims. It suggests that these claims are binding whether I like it or not. A moral law is a function of a reality, the reality of other creatures with their rights and needs, that isn't simply at my disposal.

There are different kinds of moral language. Some moral claims have to do with excellence of character, for instance, or with individual acts which it might be good to perform but which aren't obligatory. But some more claims are *peremptory*—they have overriding force. The language of law captures the force of these claims. It tells us, uncompromisingly, *Don't murder. Don't commit adultery*.

The language of law also emphasizes the consistent, patterned character of moral reason and discourse. Many moral judgments are situation specific. But to speak of moral obligation in the language of law is to emphasize the fact that there are common features of human experience that recur repeatedly. Of course, many general principles admit of exceptions, though I think that not all do. There are, I think, some absolutes. *Don't kill purposefully* is a good example. But even where we do acknowledge exceptions to general principles, that doesn't change the fact that these principles *are* generally applicable. We don't simply say: *Keep this particular promise here and now*;

we say, *As a general rule, keep promises.* We assume that there are moral constants, interests and needs that obtain in many different situations.

So the language of law is helpful when we talk about moral responsibility. It emphasizes a divine challenge to do justice that is especially important today, even if, to all appearances, ignored and forgotten. Consider the Ten Commandments, among the most profound expressions of morality in the Bible. Today, in a world gone made, the Decalogue's call to avoid murder and robbery, its challenge to be faithful to our commitments and to remember those who have gone before us and whose examples and traditions we find it easy to ignore, to avoid the dishonest misuse of legal processes, to refrain from invoking God in support of our own private agendas, to relinquish the idolatry of national pride—all seem profoundly relevant. Today, especially, the moral insights these commands contain, the peremptory demand that we attend to the suffering Other to which their form as *law* points, their independence of our wills, the fact that their general form makes it difficult to evade their impact—all make them, in the psalmist's words, more precious than gold.

9
The Ten Commandments and War in the Middle East

To speak of God's "law" is, of course, to speak metaphorically. There are numerous differences between human laws and the absolute moral norms we sometimes speak of as "the law of God," not least that human laws are *chosen*, while the moral law is simply *given*, part of the nature of reality. God can't *decide* to make torture obligatory and compassion wrong, any more than God could decide to change the rules of logic or mathematics. But to speak of God's law is to capture the objectivity, the overriding character, and the constancy of certain basic moral norms.

Some of those norms are among those expressed in the Ten Commandments. I want to suggest that we would do well to pay close attention to these profound and powerful injunctions. For there is a reasonable case to be made that, as it continues to make war in the Middle East, the US government may not be taking the principles expressed in the Ten Commandments with sufficient seriousness.

The First and Second Commandments call us to say *no* to idolatry. God alone is absolute. God alone is the center of value. God's perfection, infinity, absoluteness relativize the claim of every finite thing. To give absolute loyalty to my family, my church, my nation, myself is precisely what it means to be an idolater. What's wrong with idolatry isn't that it shortchanges God: God is infinite; God doesn't need our flattery; the divine life is enriched whenever creatures flourish and are happy. No, what's wrong with idolatry is that it necessarily involves failing to give some of God's creatures their due in order to further the interests of others. When people violate treaty obligations and wage aggressive war—risking the lives of tens, perhaps hundreds, of thousands of people on both sides, wreaking widespread destruction and economic loss, subordinating the interests of ordinary people to their own perceived strategic goals—they are, in effect, idolaters.

The Third Commandment calls us to avoid misusing God's name. Whenever we claim God as the guarantor or underwriter of our own projects, whenever we identify what we are doing with what God is doing so closely that we become God's instruments or agents, we violate this commandment. Those who employ the rhetoric of faith to justify a new crusade in the Middle East run the risk of falling foul of the Third Commandment.

The idea and experience of Sabbath say many things. But they say, among other things, that work and economic life aren't all important. By calling us to rest, to say no to work, it reminds us that making money isn't the most important thing there is. It calls into question, therefore, the rapacity of those who wish to plunder Iraq's oil reserves to line their own pockets.

Consider the Fifth Commandment, which calls us to honor our parents. Our American mothers and fathers talked a great deal about peace and justice and liberty. Much of this talk was insincere and even the sincere bits were concerned, often, with liberty, peace, and justice for *some*. Still, we do not honor them when we ignore the best ideas that form part of our heritage. We do not honor their legacy when we decline to sustain the diplomatic institutions they created (whatever their actual intentions in bringing those institutions into being). We do not honor this legacy, either, when we allow the freedoms they claimed to value to be eroded in the interests of an ill-defined security that is seen as justifying the repression of those who refuse to tow the party line. Of course, the Fifth Commandment's focus is not on honoring the memory of our forebears in just this way, but I do not think we depart radically from its spirit if we note that it calls into question the US government's rejection of the best of the American heritage.

The Sixth Commandment enjoins us not to murder. We know, I believe, that one may sometimes accept as legitimate the death of another as the foreseen but unsought outcome of one's action. But we may never murder: that is to say, we may never *intend* the death of another, seeking it purposefully or instrumentally, nor may we bring about another's death because we've taken a risk the Golden Rule would disallow. We may never impose on another a risk of death (or injury) we would not be willing to accept under similar circumstances for our loved ones or ourselves. Can American leaders truly say they have kept this commandment as they rain down death upon homes and shops and wedding parties? An attack that fails to discriminate sufficiently between combatants and noncombatants, that causes serious risk of serious injury to the latter, seems painfully inconsistent with the Sixth Commandment.

As originally understood, the Seventh Commandment addressed men: it called them not to "steal" the wives of other men, who were thought of as their husbands' property. But there are deeper underlying principles contained in this commandment, principles we can and must affirm even if we no longer think of women as men's chattels. One of these is the principle of trustworthiness, of fidelity. When I give my word, I need good reason—depending on the nature of my promise, *extremely* good reason—to break it. The US government led out in the formulation of the post-World War II international order. Americans facilitated the trial of German and Japanese leaders for waging aggressive war. And American leaders crafted and endorsed the United Nations charter, thus rejecting war as an instrument of government policy. No treaty can or should prevent people from acting to defend themselves or the victim of another's attack. But a nondefensive attack, like the US government's attacks on Iraq and Afghanistan, does seem to violate the US government's promises to the world community. If you think of governments as bound by promises (this is a complicated issue that I'll ignore here), then you can see this as a kind of infidelity that might be thought, by extension, to violate the Seventh Commandment.

The Eighth Commandment calls us not to steal. It is hard not to see some of those who favor war with Iraq as disturbingly interested in access to its oil wealth. And a war designed to give the US government or its corporate cronies influence or control over others' resources comes dangerously close, at any rate, to violating the Eighth Commandment. In addition, of course, many Americans opposed and continue to oppose war in the Middle East—and yet are compelled to help pay for it. Taking their resources against their will, under threat of force, to fund the war seems like a paradigmatic instance of theft, and so, again, inconsistent with this precept.

Originally, the Ninth Commandment would have been understood as concerned with false oaths in court. But we can see it as concerned more broadly with the manipulation of the judicial process and with the use of deception to control others. Making apparently misleading or unsupported claims about, for instance, the nature of Iraq's threats to its neighbors, the state of its weapons program, and the likely consequences of war for the Middle East and the world comes close, at any rate, to manipulative deception. And perhaps the cynical way in which those promoting war attempted to use the United Nations Security Council for their own purposes—taking the Council seriously until it became clear that the international community was simply unprepared to endorse a precipitous rush to war—also bears some analogies with the abuse of the judicial process the Ninth Commandment condemns.

The Tenth Commandment urges us not to covet. We rightly discern in this commandment a pointer to the need to avoid allowing greed for what belongs to others to lead us to engage in injustice. To the extent that American leaders act out of a desire for global power and wealth as they attack Iraq, they violate this commandment as well.

It is perhaps too much to hope that politicians should embody in their lives the principles of justice with any consistency. Especially, however, when some American leaders argue for the importance of religious language on American coins and in American schoolrooms, it is perhaps not out of place to ask that they give some thought to the call to integrity, fairness, and compassion reflected in the Decalogue. By God's grace, may they do so. And may we help them to heed God's call.

10
Faith and Faithlessness

"If we are faithless, he remains faithful—for he cannot deny himself." The claim is overwhelming. For who among us has not been faithless? How often have we betrayed our parents or our children, our churches or our communities, our partners or ourselves? It almost seems too coy to say, "If we are faithless." For we all have said no when yes would have been the right thing to say. We have all given up when we should have held on.

We also know what it is for others to be faithless. Because we are flawed, friends may shun us, lovers reject us, parents disown us. Constrained by limited resources or conflicting demands, people who care about us may be unable to keep their promises. Politicians paint glowing pictures of rosy futures only to leave office having done what politicians usually do—enrich themselves and their cronies.

And thus the remarkable quality of this declaration in 2 Timothy: "If we are faithless, he remains faithful—for he cannot deny himself." Other people may be unfaithful to us because we are flawed, because we seem unlovely, because we are too much trouble. But, proclaims 2 Timothy, God isn't like that. God isn't like that at all.

What this passage asserts in the abstract, Luke 17 displays in concrete narrative form. One leper returns to thank Jesus for healing him. The others are too preoccupied to be grateful. Jesus is too human, too vulnerable, not to ask after them. Have they forgotten him in their haste to show themselves to the priests and return to their families? Perhaps. But he has not premised his love on the demand that they be grateful, and he does not even stop to rebuke them. "If we are faithless, he remains faithful."

Second Timothy equivocates, first maintaining that God will deny us before moving on to its ringing affirmation of faithful divine love. So, too, the psalmist is not, perhaps, quite sure of God's unconditional love. His doubt—and remember that this is the psalmist's prayer, not

God's announcement—is evident when he says: "If I had cherished iniquity in my heart, the Lord would not have listened." Nonetheless, he also declares that God has not "removed his steadfast love from me!" It is this steadfast love—faithfulness despite our infidelity—that can and must be the bedrock of our confidence.

Unconditional love is no excuse for indolence or irresponsibility. Bad behavior has consequences for ourselves and for others—and so, too, for God. Recall Jeremiah's words to Jewish exiles. He urges them to be at home in a strange land. Jeremiah and many of his contemporaries interpreted the exile as a result of Israel's sin or even as divine judgment upon that sin. However we analyze the sources of the exile, Jeremiah's point remains clear: God's love is part of our lives even when we suffer divine judgment, even when we bear the consequences of our own irresponsible or hurtful actions.

That's the difference between unconditional love and cheap grace. What makes cheap grace cheap is that it denies reality. It pretends that hurtful things haven't happened. It denies that people have to take responsibility for their actions. What's wrong with cheap grace is that it isn't gracious enough. It isn't gracious to those we've hurt to deny that we need to make amends. And it isn't gracious to us to help us escape from reality. To say that God loves us unconditionally is to say that God *loves* us no matter what, not that God is an indulgent grandparent no matter what. And to love us passionately and intensely is to draw us toward excellence, toward wholeness, toward a place where we can develop and display our own capacity to love. When we experience love, we receive the gift of a profound sense of security. But at the same time we are never coddled when what we need is to be stimulated or called to account.

Unconditional love is powerful. Our great task, the task to which the Gospel calls us, is coming to grips with the reality that we are loved by God no matter what. "If we are faithless, he is faithful—for he cannot deny himself." God is love. Rejection is absolutely alien to who God is. We cannot be sure of everything this means. But as we look at our own feeble attempts to love others and accept their love, we find at least intermittent hints. As John Greenleaf Whittier wrote in "The Eternal Goodness": ""Not mine to look where cherubim / And seraphs may not see, / But nothing can be good in Him / Which evil is in me."

Our own best efforts at love provide us with faint clues to what God's love must be like. As we embrace that love, we will know ourselves secure on the granite foundation of grace. And, in turn, we will be able to experience the love of others, and give in turn to them, with greater freedom and compassion. Secure in God, we can accept their gifts without idolizing them, expecting them to offer truly godlike, perfect love to us. And, secure in God, we can attempt to offer to them our own analogue of God's unconditional love.

Conditions seem so often to be attached to people's love. Demands are placed on us, demands that we suppress who we really are to be accepted. The messages we hear suggest that conformity is the price of love. So we find it easy to feel "a deep hunger" to be free of the restraints we have internalized, a hunger "to 'just be.'" The more experiences of conditional love we have, the more burdens we bear without knowing that there is somewhere we can truly call home, truly be welcomed as we are, "the more we ache to be loved for who we are rather than what we do." Our "longing," psychiatrist Gerald May says, "goes so deep that I have never met a person who could not be moved to tears by the full realization of it."

Thus, unconditional love is an enormously valuable gift to offer another human being. But we often seem to think that love means coddling, and that demanding accountability means threatening love's withdrawal. For instance: a self-proclaimed ethics expert, speaking on an LA news station, devoted much of his five-minute spot to challenging the value of unconditional love. We may give children a free pass, he suggested, but where adult relationships are concerned we need to think of love as having conditions attached. His intentions were good, I think. He wanted to remind us of our responsibilities to the people we love. Taking someone we purport to love for granted—or worse—is a sign that we're in trouble, morally and spiritually. But that doesn't mean that we should love our partners, our children, our parents, our close friends conditionally.

Several years ago, I heard two of the three co-hosts of a drive-time radio talk show lambasting the other co-host because, while he complained about the abuse to which his father had subjected him as a child, he still bought his parents gifts and celebrated Christmas with them. In part, their concern, again, was sensible. They wondered if their friend was being hypocritical. They doubted his motives. They may have been right in part. *And yet I'm sure this man was doing the right thing.* He didn't delude himself into thinking his father's behavior had been appropriate. But he could still forgive his father and try, if only at a distance, to offer him love and respect. Even the hurtful and the destructive deserve our love. That doesn't mean, of course, that we should naïvely make ourselves their victims. Unconditional love doesn't mean leaving the embezzler free to rifle through the cash box, or assigning the molester to lead the Scout troop. It does mean continuing to acknowledge the value, the need, the vulnerability even of those whose brokenness leads them to add to the brokenness of others.

If we are faithless, God is faithful. This is good news if anything is. It calls us to return, unbidden, to acknowledge our healing like the Samaritan leper—an outsider, cherished even though he didn't belong to the "in group." It calls us to love even the ungrateful nine who fail to return. It does not encourage us to pretend that our sins don't hurt us or other people—and so God. It does not encourage us to paper over the harm we or others do, to refuse accountability ourselves or shield others from taking responsibility. But it does tell us that, whatever we do, what matters most is who we are as God's infinitely precious creatures. It invites us to bask in the rich assurance that whatever happens, we are at home in God.

11
Farewell to Retribution

As the murderous rocks rain down on him, Stephen says, "Lord Jesus, receive my spirit" (Acts 7:59). These words clearly evoke the Third Gospel's version of the crucifixion story, in which Jesus says: "Father, into your hands I commend my spirit" (Luke 23:46). And *these* words, in turn, are quoted from Psalm 31: "Into your hands I commit my spirit" (31:5).

Stephen also prays, "Lord, do not hold this sin against them" (7:60). We hear in this prayer an echo of the one Jesus speaks in Luke's account of his crucifixion: "Father, forgive them, for they do not know what they are doing" (Luke 23:34).

But notice: while Luke depicts Jesus as addressing his words to the One he cherished as "Father," Stephen speaks in almost identical terms to *Jesus*. One message in Luke's story: early Christians have already begun to think and talk about Jesus in ways previously reserved for God. The Jesus who sought God's forgiveness for others is now the object of petitions for forgiveness. The focus on forgiveness is a key difference from the sentiment we encounter in, for instance, Psalm 31. "I hate those who cling to worthless idols" (Psalm 31:6), the psalmist says. He celebrates the fact that God "pays back in full" those who are proud (Psalm 31:23). And he asks that those he calls "the wicked" be put to shame and lie silent in the grave" (Psalm 31:17).

It's not difficult to understand his reaction. He is a victim of conspiracy and slander (31:13). A trap has been set for him (31:4). His enemies' assaults have left him a pathetic object of contempt (31:11). He reacts with a painfully familiar passion for retaliation.

It will not do for those of us who aren't in pain to dismiss the psalmist's reaction too quickly. We know that we ourselves have felt the kind of anger he describes. Like him, we have hoped for the opportunity to take vengeance on those who have treated us unjustly. Our anger has burned hot, just like his.

The desire for vengeance is common—so common that we find it clearly expressed in some passages in the Bible. But we can see, if we stop to think about it, that the idea of retribution that seems to provide support for this desire doesn't make any sense. If I unjustly cause you to lose something that is purely instrumental in value, purely monetary in worth, then I can compensate you for this loss by providing you with a replacement or substitute or simply by giving you the monetary equivalent of what I have caused you to lose. What matters is not that I have lost something in the process but that you have been made whole.

When we seek revenge, when we pursue retribution or retaliation, we are seeking to repair our fragile egos. Think about our reactions to experiences of violation: so often, we are not content with compensation; we react not only out of loss but also out of humiliation and dishonor acknowledged. That is why, I think, the desire for revenge is so strong and so unaffected by reason.

The idea of retribution transplants ways of reasoning that seem appropriate in the economic sphere into non-economic sectors of our lives. We sometimes speak of retribution as a matter of compensation. But this is a case of metaphorical language doing work that ought to be done by careful argument. The idea of punishment for moral wrong means causing some harm to me because I have caused some supposedly equivalent harm to you. But it is easy to see that, once stripped of the support provided to this idea by out-of-place economic metaphors, it is fundamentally nonsensical. If I tell lies about you to our mutual friends, the harm I've done is clear: I've caused you (perhaps) to lose one or more important close relationships. The logic of retribution suggests that I should suffer some harm as a result. It is obvious, however, that no harm I might suffer could itself restore your relationship with any friend from whom you've become alienated because of my deception. You are no better off after I have been harmed than you were before.

The desire to strike back is strong, even if it's irrational. But we don't find it in what Stephen says at the end of Acts 7. Instead, Stephen models a passionate Christian commitment to forgiveness.

Like those of other martyrs, his story challenges us to do the same. What made and makes the difference between the psalmist's understandable anger and Stephen's surprising generosity of spirit? I think we can find clues in his final words: "Lord Jesus, receive my spirit."

Begin with the way Stephen invokes the risen Christ: "Lord Jesus." As I've already noted, Stephen uses language used elsewhere to address *God* to speak to *Jesus*. The use of the word "Lord" for Jesus by the early Christians points to their belief in his exalted status; *kyrios*, the Greek word translated "Lord," was used in the Septuagint for God. Jesus, the early church was increasingly convinced, had a status and authority appropriate only for God. The early church's understanding of Jesus' identity comes to expression in the Fourth Gospel's "farewell discourse." As they believe in God, they should also believe in him. To see him is to see the One he calls "Father." They should come to identify him as the human face of God (14:9).

This means that, as they recalled Jesus' forgiveness of his enemies, the early Christians could not help but affirm that God was a forgiver. The God who is at the heart of all things is visible in the image of a bruised and broken man begging for mercy for those who have hurt him. If God looks like this, how could Stephen not respond with mercy to his attackers? How can he not echo the words of the one he acclaims as Lord? If it is the risen Jesus to whom he prays, how can his sentiments be other than those of this same Jesus on the cross?

His followers' identification of Jesus as God's presence in our world meant that in *his* love they discerned *God's* love. They not only remembered a forgiveness they believed themselves to model, but also felt themselves embraced by a love which offered them a liberating security. "Do not let your hearts be troubled," Jesus says in John 14, urging his disciples to trust him. He says, metaphorically, that he "goes to prepare a place" for his friends (John 14:1, 2). He offers them home. Similarly, 1 Peter emphasizes the sense of calling, of belonging, enjoyed by the early Christians. Those who were formerly outsiders now have a home: they have been "called . . . out of darkness and into . . . [God's] marvelous light." They are now "the people of God," the recipients of mercy (1 Peter 2:9-10).

Having a place to call home, knowing oneself welcomed by a warm embrace, is a profound source of security, one that can free us from self-concern. The Christian rejection of vengeance is *justified* by the fact that the idea of retribution is senseless. It is *modeled* by Jesus' own practice of forgiveness. But perhaps at least sometimes it is *inspired* and *empowered* by the security that comes from an awareness of divine love—an awareness fostered by, among other things, our encounter with that love in the story of Jesus. Knowing ourselves grounded, knowing our identities secure, does not remove the need to protect others and ourselves from evil. But perhaps it can sometimes help us move beyond the impulse to protect our egos and respond retributively to humiliation and dishonor. Perhaps, sometimes, it can help to heal our wounds and free us from the need to lash out at our enemies.

At a time of brutal violence, when the land where Stephen died is covered with the blood of Jews and Arabs alike, when the raw wound left by the September 11 terrorist attack has yet to heal, when violence is a fact of daily life, we need anew to hear the words of Stephen. "Receive my spirit," he prays, confident in a God who is present and active in his life even in the midst of senseless atrocities. "Receive my spirit"—as if to say, *I want to come home to you, to you with whom I am already at home.* May we share this sense of being at home in and with a God who embraces us, a God we can discern in the figure of Jesus, praying for his enemies as they torture him. May we find the grace to join with Stephen in praying, "Lord, do not hold this sin against them."

12
Power and Violence

En route to Jerusalem, according to the Third Gospel, James and John decide that the time for violence is long overdue. Residents of a Samaritan village refuse to welcome Jesus—after all, he's headed for the principal city of the Samaritans' religious rivals—and the disciples sometimes called the "Sons of Thunder" see violence as a natural response. "Master," they ask, "do you want us to call fire down from heaven to destroy them?"

It is interesting to ask just what they have in mind. When I first read about the violent, apocalyptic fantasies of the members of the Qumran community, who gave us the Dead Sea scrolls, I assumed that they believed God would actually rain down death on their enemies from heaven. Divine miracles would annihilate the Romans and those who collaborated with them, along with the impure and unholy. And perhaps that's what they envisioned. But I've realized that when the biblical prophets talk about God's action in history, they're thinking of mediated action, action occurring in and through the acts of human beings. So I have come to wonder whether the War Scroll of the Essenes might not have depicted what the Essenes themselves hoped God would do to their enemies *through them*. They may truthfully have believed that they were referring to God's work, while understanding that the work would be performed by human hands.

Thinking in this way, I cannot help but wonder when I read this passage whether the earliest readers might have understood James and John to have had in mind divine judgment rendered by human hands—not, perhaps, under Roman rule, but rather, say, at the time when, under the messianic leadership they may have supposed Jesus would provide for a rebellion, Israel's people had begun to control their own land again.

This is obviously pure speculation. What is not speculation is that, as they are depicted in this story of their call for a downpouring of fire, James and John believe that God is a God of vengeance and that divine justice is rightly meted out to those who put false religious beliefs on display. More broadly, they believe that God is a god of power. The author of Second Kings similarly conceives of God as materializing a chariot of fire and horses of fire and uses a whirlwind to draw Elijah into heaven. The images of the fire, the horses, and the whirlwind all suggest raw, untamable power, and Second Kings seeks to highlight God's possession and use of such power.

The same vision is evident in the words of the psalmist, who celebrates God's "mighty deeds," the "wonders of old" accomplished by God's power. Superior to the other gods, Yahweh puts divine might on display in view of the world's people, instilling terror even in the waters of chaos. Israel's god is a warrior, whose arrows are lightning bolts, and who works redemption by violence.

There is a stark contrast between the posture of James and John and the way of life commended in Galatians by Paul. The Golden Rule's requirement of fairness and a ringing call to bear the Spirit's harvest in one's own life—a harvest of love, joy, peace, patience, kindness, goodness, faithfulness, gentleness and self-control—are nothing like the program of divine vengeance the disciples seek to foster or implement.

Ironically, however, today, in a society awash in Christian imagery, the god of power clearly takes precedence over the God who nurtures the flowering of fairness and grace. Punishment, retaliation, retribution—these are regularly sought not only by demagogues but by people steeped in traditions of peace (like the gentle Quaker radio commentator whose jarring call for a post-September 11 invasion of Afghanistan I still recall with dismay). Like James and John, good people today call down fire out of heaven, sometimes all too literally.

More broadly, though, power—sometimes therapeutic, sometimes paternalistic—is increasingly pervasive. It may not come to expression in overt acts of violence. But as people's lives are regimented, manipulated, structured, corralled, subjected to surveillance, as due process is increasingly treated as a relic of the past (all this as people relish each year's ritual sermonizing about freedom), we see a disturbingly familiar model of power put more and more confidently on display. It does not always feature the overt violence about which

James and John enthuse in our Gospel—though some times it does. But it involves the same implacable willingness to ride rough-shod over dissent, even if clothed, often enough, in a friendlier visage. The road ahead is paved with easy slogans and good intentions.

It is easy for us comfortably to indulge in a sense of self-righteous superiority, knowing ourselves to be peaceful and tolerant. We don't celebrate or call for punitive violence, do we?

Well, do we?

I suspect our attitudes are often more punitive than we would like to think. It's surprisingly easy for decent people to decide that a colleague who has messed up in some way ought to be sent packing—not because they expect more bad things from her or him in the future, but as retribution for past behavior (or to convey a message of moral rectitude to the community).

But let's grant that we aren't always punitive. We can still find ways, institutionally and personally, to control and dominate. Emotional manipulation of our loved ones, paternalistic attempts to manage others' lives for their own good, decisions rooted in the serene confidence that we know what's best for others, whatever their own preferences—none of these things involves a call for fire to come down out of heaven, but all of them reflect a willing embrace of power.

Recall that James and John's horrific proposal to Jesus comes as he is proceeding to Jerusalem for a final confrontation with those who hold the reins of power in his society. That confrontation will climax as Jesus hangs on the cross, crying out in terror and abandonment, "My God, my God, why have you forsaken me?" Central to the Christian gospel is the attempt to rethink divine power as the power of a God seen with surprising and disturbing clarity in this image of Jesus on the cross. The impact of that image on Christians' perceptions of divine power continues to reverberate: too many people still see Jesus as a temporary disguise for the god of power, the god who calls down fire. But the deification of oppressive power is difficult, at best, to square with support for the Golden Rule and the harvest of the Spirit.

We can see that. But seeing the truth doesn't free us from inner conflict. To use the language of Paul's letter to the Galatians: the sinful nature—the side of us that seeks aggressive power, that relishes domination—struggles against the Spirit, and the Spirit nudges and lures and woos us toward a way of life in contrast to the authoritarianism craved by the sinful nature. We have work to do, in our own lives, and in the institutions and communities we influence.

Elijah spoke truth to power (even if he, too, seems to have embraced a picture of God as identified with aggressive force). We, too, can speak truth to power (including our own). We can say "no" to the temptation to call down fire out of heaven, "no" to the temptation to celebrate domination and control and the kind of imperial authority that crucified Jesus once he reached Jerusalem. Let's remember that we, and all people, are called to be free, and to love.

13
The Exodus Legacy

"If slavery is not wrong, nothing is wrong," Abraham Lincoln wrote in 1864. Christian defenders of slavery offered biblical arguments for their position, and those arguments may have been plausible on fundamentalist premises. But abolitionism (with which Lincoln, more interested in preserving the Union at all costs than in ending slavery, had a rather complicated relationship) resonated with a deeply rooted element of the Jewish and Christian heritage. Christianity is grounded in Judaism, and the people Israel remembers itself as ultimately a community of freed slaves.

As political theorist Michael Walzer has reminded us, the story of the Exodus has inspired successive generations of revolutionaries. Victims of Jim Crow in the South of the 1960s found hope and challenge in the tale of an earlier generation's triumph over oppression. Oliver Cromwell told his fellow Puritans to look to the Exodus as a model. John Calvin and John Knox drew on the Exodus to validate their political choices. Benjamin Franklin thought the Exodus provided a pattern for early America. Karl Marx referred to it as well.

It's hard to overestimate the significance of the Exodus story for our culture, and for our religious convictions. It has served as a perennial reminder of the central Jewish and Christian conviction that God is on the side of the oppressed and enslaved, that those without power can look to God for deliverance. We can reasonably seeing it as unleashing a new dynamic in world history, a dynamic responsible for an increasing resistance to an authority and a growing awareness of the fundamental equality of persons. The seeds planted by the Exodus obviously didn't take root all at once. The people Israel had slaves. And the book of Joshua remembers them as having acted as brutal oppressors themselves in Canaan. But the Exodus changed everything, as perhaps no other event in western religious history other than the life of Jesus has done.

Vulnerability and Community

With only a little stretching, we can perhaps even see the commitment to freedom and equality released into history by the Exodus story at work in Romans. Obviously, there are more immediately relevant factors—notably the story of Jesus itself, the dangerous memory of his open and inclusive love. But, of course, the Exodus shaped the culture in which God's revelation in the Jesus story took place. It is not absurd, I think, to see the image of a community of equals birthed by the Exodus as one of the influences on Paul's call to the weak and the strong to avoid offending or condemning each other. Paul is clearly "of the strong"—confident of his liberation in Christ, he knows himself not bound by many traditional taboos, even if he has not yet found release from all. But he wants the church at Rome to be a place where all Christians can feel at home, where judgment and condemnation and rejection are absent.

This spirit is continuous with that of the Exodus: Paul seeks freedom, equal dignity, and community for all Christians, exhibiting genuine continuity with the Exodus story. But Paul strikes a note in Romans 14 that seems absent from the Exodus story itself, as conventionally remembered—a note of inclusiveness and acceptance, of openness to the other person who is different, surprising, unsettling, annoying. For all the liberating power of the story, for all its justified outrage at oppression and its passion for deliverance, those who have told it have often been tempted to a one-sided view of things. Consider the way it's handled in Psalm 114. While the psalmist refers to Israel's deliverance from Egypt and depicts the confrontation at the sea, she or he explicitly notes only the movement of the water. There is no reference to the Egyptians drowned beneath the flood.

The Exodus story is not like the later tales of the conquest of Canaan: it is not a story of rapacious plunder, genocide, and massacre. Here, Israel is clearly in the right. Jacob's descendants have been enslaved; they are rightly fleeing from slavery; and they would surely be justified in responding directly with limited force to their pursuing oppressors. But despite the injustice of the Egyptians and the justice of Israel's cause, the humanity of the Egyptians still matters. One of the biggest temptations for people who are being treated unjustly is to assume that their oppression makes it OK for them to treat their oppressors as if the oppressors' humanity no longer mattered (and, for that matter, to ignore their own capacity to *be* oppressors).

In this respect, they're rather like the ungrateful servant in the familiar gospel story. Released from a crushing debt, he is unable to see a fellow servant who owes *him* money as a person in need. He is aware only of his own desires and needs. His own perspective overwhelms the other's.

Oppressed people often, to be sure, have a good excuse: when you're a victim of injustice—and few injustices are worse than the slavery to which the people Israel are subjected in Egypt—you need to fight hard just to keep your spirits and your self-respect alive. It's hard to find room in your imagination for the face of the oppressor. It's important to concentrate your energy, focus your will, muster all the determination available to you as you seek to resist. Hatred is a powerful motivator; resisting evil is easier if you identify your concrete, flesh-and-blood opponents with the evil they're doing *without remainder*, if you treat them as if not just particular things they've done or are doing but they themselves are *evil incarnate*. It's easier if you pretend that they're not persons.

But that, I think, is what Paul challenges us *not* to do in Romans 14. He calls Christians in Rome to see that those with whom they disagree are also children of God, to find ways of being open to otherness, to avoid judgment and condemnation. "Let us," he says, "stop passing judgment on one another." That doesn't mean that everything is relative, that all positions are equally acceptable. Paul is one of the "strong"; on his view, the "weak" to whom he refers are, objectively speaking, unequivocally mistaken. But that doesn't mean the personhood of the weak doesn't matter. We sometimes hear calls not to judge, implying that we ought not to discriminate between good and evil; I think that's not the point here. Rather, Paul's vision of inclusive love calls us to accept and care for *people* even as we reject and condemn their *unjust actions*.

We are heirs of the Exodus. This powerful story of freedom challenges us to participate in the work of human liberation. We are heirs of Jesus and Paul. Their vision of inclusive community, their rejection of judgmentalism, challenges us to see the genuine humanity of those we oppose as we seek to end injustice—in our personal lives or in the public world. The racist official who seeks to prevent the integration of a public school is doing something evil that ought resolutely to be opposed—but that makes him no less a person, no less God's child. The corporate executive who robs shareholders and deceives and degrades employees needs to be challenged unequivocally—but that doesn't mean her own personhood and value can be written off. The church or university administrator who stands in the way of positive change may be dead wrong, but that doesn't make her or him an embodiment of evil, to be opposed with venom and contempt. The government official who plots a dangerous and destructive war may be doing something that violates two millennia of Christian teaching about justice in war, but she or he remains a real, valuable person, embraced by God's love.

Let's celebrate God's liberating Exodus work, then, remembering Israel's deliverance. At the same time, let's remember a God of infinite forgiveness and boundlessly inclusive love who accepts us despite our brokenness and evil and calls us, in turn, to remember with love the humanity even of those whose injustice we unswervingly condemn.

14
On Being Good Shepherds

"We are . . . [God's] people, the sheep of . . . [God's] pasture." These words immediately follow the psalmist's injunction to "worship . . . [God] with gladness," and they precede the call to give thanks to a God whose "love endures forever." Thinking of God as a shepherd, and so of ourselves as sheep, might not strike all of us as cause for joy. We think of sheep us unintelligent, and we may well not want to be compared with them. And we may well not want the kind of direction a shepherd might need to give a flock of foolish and unruly sheep. But the image of God's care as that of a considerate shepherd could clearly be a comforting one under the right circumstances—as, for instance, in Israel at the time of Ezekiel.

Power, Lord Acton famously said, tends to corrupt. Ezekiel would have agreed. He noted with frustration in Ezekiel 34 that those who should have cared for Israel—its shepherds—looked out only for their own interests. "You eat the curds, clothe yourselves with the wool and slaughter the choice animals, but you do not take care of the flock. You have not strengthened the weak or healed the sick or bound up the injured. You have not brought back the strays or searched for the lost. You have ruled them harshly and brutally" (Ez. 34:3-4). The irresponsible leadership of Israel's elites had resulted in the scattering of the flock entrusted to their care. God would need to rescue the lost sheep, to "bring them out from the nations and gather them from the countries [of their exile], and . . . into their own land." God would need to do justice, to deal with the consequences of the unjust self-enrichment of some at the expense of others. (It is hard not to see the metaphors shifting here, to see those spoken of as the irresponsible shepherds at the beginning of Ezekiel 34 described in verses 20-24 as the "fat sheep" who butt "all the weak sheep with . . . [their] horns.) God's leadership is contrasted with that of irresponsible leaders who abuse their power. The image of a shepherd who searches for the lost, binds up the injured, and strengthens the weak serves to highlight the rapacious oppressiveness of Israel's ruling class.

This is not necessarily the most obvious way to look at social, political, and economic power. When Andrew Jackson became president of the United States, he famously defended his decision to replace those who had held a wide variety of government posts under his predecessor with his own cronies and loyalists by saying, "To the victor belong the spoils!" Many people view politics as a game that gives those in the power the right to use their influence, authority, and positions to enrich themselves and their supporters. But Ezekiel offers a very different image of leadership. Being a leader doesn't mean being entitled to enrich yourself at the expense of the vulnerable. Rather, it means taking responsibility for protecting the vulnerable—taking care of the flock, strengthening the weak, healing the sick, binding up the injured, bringing back the strays, searching for the lost. And this, we have to acknowledge, is not, in fact, what states do as a matter of course. Instead, they use their power to enrich entrenched elites at the expense of ordinary people. And this is not a problem to be fixed by replacing one set of politicians with another, both because the sorts of people who become successful politicians are likely to be ambitious and greedy and because those who occupy government positions consistently confront powerful temptations to benefit themselves and their cronies.

Ezekiel rejects this kind of abuse: God will, he says, "destroy" "the sleek and the strong." The vision of inclusive love we derive from Jesus rightly makes us uncomfortable with the view that even those who have grown sleek and strong by oppression will be destroyed: they, too, are God's children. But the work of justice surely must mean restoring and empowering the vulnerable, and therefore *reducing* the power of those who have profited by injustice. This is simply an expression of the fundamental conviction that persons are equal in value and moral status implicit in that same vision of inclusive love—in the injunction to do unto others as we would be done by, to love our neighbors as ourselves. And those in power may regard the restoration of equality as an assault on their personhood tantamount to destruction. Even if we question the aptness of Ezekiel's choice of images, then, we can see the value of a restorative justice that deals in dramatic and decisive ways with the consequences of oppression.

It is to a model of leadership to which concern for this kind of justice is central that the story of Jesus calls us. Early Christians could speak metaphorically of the risen Christ as "head over everything," as does Ephesians 1. Whatever else this language does, it certainly calls our attention to Jesus as a source of insight into the practice of leadership. The Ephesian Christians are spoken of as exhibiting "faith in the Lord Jesus Christ." Just a few years after his death, Jesus of Nazareth was being described as an object of faith. Jesus was seen in intimate relation to God, even if the early Christians weren't certain how best to describe that relationship and would spend centuries attempting to clarify their thinking. But if faith in the person of Jesus was appropriate, then Jesus could surely be understood—I think they would have said—as revealing God, as a window on the character of God. Jesus' vision of leadership, of authority, can be seen as illuminating God's.

Consider Matthew 25, then. Here, Jesus seems to draw on a theme familiar from Israel's history—in Ezekiel and elsewhere—of the king as shepherd and of God as the true shepherd who does what Israel's royal shepherds can or will not do. Like Ezekiel, he condemns disregard for the weak, the vulnerable, the poor, emphasizing that disregard for his followers, even at their weakest, is ultimately disregard for himself. The image of the leader here is of someone concerned with justice—and with justice understood specifically as care for the vulnerable, the imprisoned, the oppressed.

The biblical witness to God's love repeatedly stresses the importance of imitating God. And the prophetic vision of history suggests clearly, if not unequivocally, that God's activity in the world is mediated activity, activity that takes place in and through the activity of creatures. When Ezekiel speaks of God as doing justice, we should recognize, I think, that God is understood to foster justice in our world by means of human institutions and social processes. Humans are called to imitate God in the world—and so to be the ones who enact God's love and justice.

To take Ezekiel's vision of God's work on behalf of justice in the world as a source of inspiration for our own would mean encouraging a different kind of leadership in our communities, in our society, in our world. We cannot, should not, must not encourage leadership as domination, nonconsensual leadership, paternalistic leadership. And we will want to encourage leaders—not politicians, not bureaucrats—who are committed to binding up the injured, and who therefore seek to challenge barriers to inexpensive health care for all (barriers frequently imposed by well connected professional and industry groups). We will want to encourage leaders—not politicians, not bureaucrats—who are committed to strengthening the weak, and who therefore seek to empower by challenging the debilitating "wars" on drugs and "terror," wars that sap the vitality of so many communiites, and by increasing the diversity of educational options available to parents and students. We will want to encourage leaders—not politicians, not bureaucrats—who will work to keep those with economic and political power from stealing the property and controlling the lives of the marginal and the weak. We will understand that leaders who care about shepherding their flocks with justice will attempt to see that the vulnerable are treated as well as the powerful.

God call human leaders to exhibit the care of shepherds for their flocks, to protect and nurture the vulnerable, to empower the powerless. Our task, locally and globally, is to challenge those who lead to be good shepherds—and, where appropriate, to be good shepherds, effective leaders, ourselves. Thus, we can contribute to making God's world the kind of place for which all people can shout for joy.

15
Kings

The story of David is arguably the richest and most textured in the Bible, the one that reads the most like a good biography or a good novel. A few years ago, my wife and I watched the abortive TV series *Kings*, which recasts the story in something like the contemporary world; the series readily reminds me how naturally the biblical David narratives lend themselves to dramatic treatment, and how much nuance and complexity are already there.

David's anointing has figured in innumerable edifying discourses focused on God's attention to inward realities we may readily overlook. And I'm sure it's true that most of us need repeated reminders that what we see and what's really the case are often very much not the same thing (though it's interesting to note that the author of First Samuel makes certain to reassure us that David, too, was handsome and strong—the point is obviously not that there's anything wrong with appreciating beauty, but that we need to be careful about assuming that beauty is necessarily a mark of strength or virtue, though of course it may be). But it is perhaps too easy to think of the anointing as unequivocally A Good Thing, both for David and for Israel. Life is, I suspect, more complex than that.

In 1 Samuel, the prophet mourns Saul, his friend even if also his enemy. But the downward spiral of Saul's career should hardly be surprising. After all, Samuel has already warned that naming a king would lead to tyranny and taxation and war. Selecting a king is a bad idea; authoritarianism and extortion are the likely consequences. So Samuel can hardly have been surprised to find a king misbehaving: misbehaving is what kings do. And so, while God is said to regret having made Saul king, the forecast of kingly injustice that precedes Saul's anointing suggests what must be seen as the real point, that God must be thought of as regretting the selection of any king at all.

Unfortunately, as the Israelite leaders' words to Samuel make clear, it's all too easy to cheer for a war leader, to ignore the rampant injustice and ridiculous expense associated with war, to paper over a war leader's iniquities and inequities, to feel a rush of enthusiasm as enemies are smitten down.

But there is also another, not unrelated, problem: when a king is in office, it is easy to expect him to be successful, especially if he is the putative recipient of divine favor (as, of course, almost all kings want us to suppose they are). Think of Psalm 20's confident invocation of divine blessing on the king: "Lord, give victory to the king," the psalmist prays. And then: "The Lord gives victory to his anointed. He answers him from his heavenly sanctuary with the victorious power of his right hand."

Now, we have every reason to be queasy about the assumption that the king's enemies are God's enemies. But even outside the context of war, the notion that God will not only endorse the king's agenda but also ensure its success is troubling. Of course it's troubling because the king isn't God, and treating a human project as God's project is the essence of idolatry. But it's also troubling because, even when, in appropriately constrained and relative ways, the king seeks to do well, God is not, we know, in the business of guaranteeing success.

I suspect it is the king, and not everyone in the congregation, who is the focus of the language in Psalm 20. But the problem persists even if we understand the language more inclusively. It is easy to share the psalmist's hope that God will give us the desires of our hearts, will grant all our requests. And the psalmist's words are, if nothing else, powerful reminders of the fact that our desires are not to be squelched or silenced or ignored, that God seeks to see us fulfilled and flourishing, not as shriveled, world-denying ascetics.

Nonetheless, as Paul emphasizes, "we live by faith and not by sight." Traditionally, Psalm 20 has been attributed to David. And the stories of David we find in the books of Kings and Chronicles are stories of someone whose dreams are sometimes fulfilled more wonderfully than he could have imagined, but who in other cases finds little but dust and ashes.

If God indeed gives victory to the anointed, this cannot be a matter of some divine guarantee, *ensuring* that the king's plans will be fulfilled. David lost Saul and Jonathan, both of whom he loved, despite the conflict and desperation that persistently marred his relationship with Saul. He lost his infant son in a night of weeping, and watched his golden child, Absalom, turn against him and seek to destroy him. Friends fell in war. His wife, Michal, spurned him. He may pray, as we might pray for anyone we love, that God may give him the desires of his heart. But he can have no illusion that those desires are always granted, that God's realm will come in force in ways that will overwhelm and dominate. He will surely have hoped for divine blessing, but his own experience can have offered him little justification for supposing that God would forcibly ensure his success.

That needn't mean, of course, that God is absent from the world or that there is nothing for which to hope. But it must mean that God's presence in the world is ambiguous, that God's activity in the world is persuasive, not coercive, undertaken in and through the actions of free creatures who can say "no," of finite creatures who cannot always achieve their goals, of fallible creatures who are often disastrously wrong.

If we say, then, with Paul, that "the new creation has come. The old is gone; the new is here!," we know that this does not, cannot, mean that God has intervened to eliminate all that stands between us and the achievement of our goals. We experience a *foretaste* of a better world, not that world fully realized—a new way of being, a new style of life, a new kind of community. We see the mustard seed growing from insignificance into greatness. We see the scattered seed, growing quietly and then flowering.

Kings can't do what they say will do: they can't bring peace and prosperity, both because theirs is the way of violence and because they lack the insight, the understanding, the knowledge to do what ordinary people, linked in innumerable networks of alliance and often anonymous cooperation can accomplish. And they can't count on God to ratify their projects, both because God does not endorse the idolatrous identification of human and divine projects and because God's work in the world doesn't proceed as kings might be expected to prefer, in showy, dramatic, coercive, and overwhelming ways.

Vulnerability and Community

    Kingship isn't for celebrating. Kings are unjust. Their plans fail. Neither for themselves nor for us can they guarantee victory. And God certainly isn't in the business of vouchsafing their success. We might wish to be, as Paul says, "away from the body and at home with the Lord," with the expectation that, if we were, things might be different. But here and now, as we live in hope, not in certainty, we cannot but see that God's way is not the way of kings and that the ways of kings are not God's way and that, rather than seeking for the victories of war leaders we might do well, instead, to hope for the organic development of social life rooted in peaceful cooperation, for the flowering of the mustard seed.

16
Fishing for People

With the dynamism typical of Jesus as Mark portrays him, Simon, Andrew, James, and John are called to become "fishers of people." Jesus himself has already proclaimed the nearness of God's reign and issued a call to repentance; now, he enlists a cadre of followers in his cause. Presumably the four men he calls in Mark 1 have already become acquainted with him—perhaps simply as hearers, perhaps as conversation partners. Now, however, they accept the challenge of a new role as his coworkers.

It is easy to read the story of the call of Jesus' disciples through the lenses provided by later developments in Christian history, to hear the children's lyric, "I will make you fishers of men," as we listen to Jesus' words. But it is not clear that Jesus was seeking to recruit evangelists of the Billy Graham variety, preachers who would tell their listeners how to escape from eternal death. He was not announcing that—as some Bible translators suggest Paul was saying in 1 Corinthians 7—"the world in its present form is passing away," at least if this meant the *physical* world. Initiating what he saw as a God-inspired transformative social movement, he wanted and needed help.

When he preached that God's reign was near, he didn't mean that the end of the world was imminent, but that God was already beginning to do something dramatic in Israel's history in and through his own ministry. He wanted and needed associates who would work with him to challenge Israel to see what God was doing and to respond to and participate in God's action. And he wanted to make clear that if Israel failed to change course, it would find itself in inevitable conflict with Rome, with devastating consequences for Jerusalem and the Jewish people. Like Nineveh in the book of Jonah, Jerusalem would fall. Doom was imminent if Israel didn't change its ways.

Jesus was issuing a call to repentance. But *repentance* here didn't mean a vague call to individuals to abandon a life of sin in favor of a life of goodness. It targeted Israel as a nation, and it meant something quite specific. It meant abandoning Israel's then-characteristic attitude toward the Gentile world, marked by suspicion, exclusion, and the maintenance of rigid boundaries. And it meant abandoning the system of domination that obtained within Israelite society, marked by the spiritual and economic oppression of poor people and social outsiders. A good analogue for the role Jesus envisioned for his disciples today might be not so much *evangelist* as *activist*. (Think of those religious leaders who have helped to organize massive demonstrations in support of peace in our country as potential models.) Jesus needed helpers who would raise the collective consciousness of his contemporaries, who would help them to see that their nation needed a sharp and immediate change in direction.

Christianity's commitment to global mission has energized generations of people. It has led to the creation of vibrant, worldwide communities of faith. Too often, though, our understanding of Christian mission has focused on encouraging people to adopt the right beliefs and do the right things so they can escape the horrors of divine judgment. We've often implied that people need to be Christians for God to like them. But to say this flies in the face of the basic Jewish and Christian conviction that God is gracious. God doesn't need to be convinced to like us. The psalmist encourages us to find hope, rest, and salvation in God, a God in whom one can trust at all times, a God who is our refuge. God is strong, says the psalmist; and God is loving. A God who can be described as loving can't reasonably be seen as an arbitrary, exacting tyrant who will send people to hell because they fail to get their beliefs right.

It's certainly not easy to get this sort of conception of Christian mission from Mark's gospel. Jesus' call to repentance simply doesn't address the situation of belief change across cultures; he clearly believed that Israel's God was the God of all people, and he affirmed so-called "God-fearers," Gentiles who didn't identify with Israel ethnically or culturally but who nonetheless acknowledged the claim of Israel's God. He was no cultural relativist who assumed that any culture is as good as any other. But he does not suggest in Mark's gospel that getting one's beliefs or community identification right is the key to getting God to like us, to enjoying life beyond death, or anything similar. His focus is on the ways in which Israel, its attitudes, its structures must change.

I suggest that Jesus' own focus makes the most sense as a guide for our own. Our church can and must retain a powerful sense of mission if it is to maintain its vitality and relevance. But the purpose of its mission cannot be to persuade people to become Christian so God will like them, so God will refrain from killing them. The conviction that God doesn't love people who don't share our beliefs, that God isn't present and active in healing and redemptive ways in communities other than ours, flies in the face of the psalmist's vision of God's love and tempts us to repeat the kind of exclusivism Jesus saw as leading his nation to its doom. We would do better to adopt the same focus as Jesus. We would do better, that is, to challenge exclusion in the name of community, to challenge subordination and exploitation in the name of solidarity, social cooperation, and equality of dignity and rights.

The world needs our witness. The convictions people endorse matter for their lives and the lives of others whom they touch. But it is not with regard primarily to theological and philosophical doctrines—at least in the narrow sense—but, rather, to moral, social, and legal issues that the really challenging disagreements between religious and cultural traditions occur, and it is on these that our mission and evangelism must focus. Thus, our goal must be to challenge beliefs and practices that keep God's good creation from flourishing, rather than urging people to endorse all of our theological formulations. Instead of worrying, therefore, about preserving trivial differences from our neighbors while endorsing what's most wrong with our society uncritically, we might consider abandoning our focus on trifles and focusing on the ways in which our vision of God's universal love and our celebration of God's good creation might bring us *appropriately* into conflict with our surroundings.

Consider, for example, our witness not to some alien culture but to the world of contemporary North America. In this culture, instead of characterizing Sabbath observance as a dividing line between the saved and the unsaved, we might reasonably point to the Sabbath as an implicit condemnation of our society's idolatry of work. Work hours are increasing dramatically. People's jobs seem to demand more and more from them. And subordination and abuse at work continue. We need to announce and embody the message of the Deuteronomy 15 Sabbath command that God says no to exploitative, bad work, and the message of the Exodus 20 Sabbath command that the priority of the Creator's love means that even good work doesn't determine the meaning and value of our lives.

Similarly, instead of arguing about the *how* of God's creative work, we might do well to stress that, because God is the world's creator, God cannot simply be the tribal deity of our nation or culture. Ours is a global church community; and the doctrine of God's creatorship we affirm should challenge us to be loyal not only to this or that community but also, and most importantly, to the whole world. In an increasingly interconnected world, it is more and more important to stress that the Creator's love embraces all creatures, human and non-human alike. That means that we must be in the forefront of those who challenge military, diplomatic, or economic policies that treat some residents of our global village as second-class people—by denying them the freedom to immigrate and work, for instance, by keeping them from selling their products or their labor freely around the globe (because First World producers fear competition from them), or by subjecting them to violence in order to steal their property.

We can and should see our mission, then, as a matter of witness—of testifying both in the shape of our own common life and in the content of our communication with the world to the practical implications of our convictions. That's a potentially exciting and challenging mission, one that could energize Christians across the globe without trapping us in exclusivistic ghettos. And it's one that exhibits meaningful continuity, I believe, with the mission to which Mark's Jesus calls Simon, Andrew, James, and John when he urges them to become "fishers of people."

17
Jesus Was a Jew

Jesus of Nazareth died on a Roman cross, undergoing agonies reserved for provincials whom Rome saw as threatening its power. Israel's leaders had no authority from Rome to execute anyone. And those Jewish leaders who connived in his execution represented a small minority that actively oppressed ordinary Jews. But the idea that "the Jews," Jesus' own people, were primarily responsible for killing him quickly became a feature of popular Christian versions of the story of his death.

The bizarre idea that the participation of some Jewish leaders in Jesus' judicial murder somehow justified treating all Jews in successive generations as "Christ-killers" found expression in the ghettoes of the Middle Ages and afterward, and subsequently in the participation of Christians in the Holocaust. But we can hear it anticipated even in Christian texts from the first century. In the Fourth Gospel's account of Jesus' first appearance to his followers after his death, we read that the disciples have locked their doors "for fear of the Jews." In Acts, Israel's leaders argue that the disciples "are determined to bring . . . [Jesus'] blood on us," and the disciples, in effect, agree. Though these leaders lacked the right to execute anyone, and though there is no question that Rome's representatives killed Jesus, the disciples place exclusive responsibility for Jesus' death on the Jewish leaders they are addressing. "[Y]ou," they tell these leaders, "had [Jesus] killed by hanging him on a tree." It is hard not to imagine that these same leaders are in view when the Apocalypse emphasizes that "those who pierced" him will see the returning Christ, "and [that] on his account all the tribes of the earth will wail."

It is easy to see why emphasizing Jewish responsibility for Jesus' death might have made sense to the early Christians. Consider an example: Christians evidently began to abandon the observance of the Sabbath on the seventh day of the week for a simple reason: worshipping on the seventh day was a mark of affiliation with Judaism. The Romans saw Jews as troublemakers. So distancing themselves from Jews was—many early Christians must have believed—a crucial survival strategy.

Obviously, choosing to observe the Sabbath on Sunday rather than Saturday would have been only one way in which the early Christians would likely have sought to avoid the unpleasant consequences of Roman anti-Judaism. Telling the story of Jesus' death in a way that maximized Jewish responsibility and minimized Roman responsibility could well have been another. Certainly, in any case, it seems as if this is what has happened. As we read early Christian accounts of Jesus' trial and crucifixion, we can see how weight is placed on the role not only of the Jewish leaders but also, in some cases, the Jewish people as a whole, and how Rome's role is downplayed. Pilate, for instance, who seems to have been cruel and tyrannical, becomes a weak, vacillating figure swayed by Jewish pressure.

There is a certain irony here. For not only was Jesus himself a Jew, of course, but the evidence is also strong that his attitudes toward cultural boundaries and barriers helped to trigger the events that led to his death. Many of his contemporaries seemed to believe that the best way to respond to Rome's occupation and domination of Israel was to establish a social order marked by purity. It was important, from their perspective, to draw clear lines between good Jews and bad Jews and between Jews and Gentiles. Making sure that insiders stayed in and outsiders stayed out was a crucial part of the faithfulness to God that would ensure Israel's ultimate victory over its enemies.

This isn't a distinctively Jewish strategy, of course. The "politics of holiness" which Jesus confronted in his society had and has many analogues in other times and places. Numerous societies—ours included—have sought to identify insiders and outsiders and police the boundaries between them. But easy though it may be to adopt a strategy of inclusion and exclusion, Jesus rejected it. He articulated a vision of an Israel marked precisely by its permeable boundaries, by its rejection of the insider-outsider schema that treated poor Jews, women, and Gentiles as undesirable. He sought to foster the growth of a community from which no one needed to feel excluded. And his challenge to the politics of holiness almost certainly helped to precipitate his crucifixion.

As I say, then, there's an irony here. A community inspired by the practice of Jesus can hardly be a community that turns any group, perhaps especially Jesus' own people, into a collection of outsiders. Psalm 150 invites "everything that breathes" to praise God. And I think that strikes just the right note: God is open to the whole creation, seeking to embrace every living thing. And the Gospel is the message not only that we are thus embraced by a God of infinite grace but also that we can help to make God's grace tangible by being a community in which everyone is invited to feast together, in which no one is excluded from the table.

Most of us might shake our heads at the thought of Christians meeting in secret today "for fear of the Jews." But during the centuries since the death of Jesus, Jesus' own people have met behind locked doors often enough "for fear of the Christians." The complex and often painful history of Christianity's relationship with Judaism is a reminder that strategies of exclusion come all too easily to us—even, perhaps especially, those of us inclined to rail against the putative narrowness and sectarianism of others.

Desiring, as we must, to put behind us the hostility toward the people Israel that has distorted Jewish-Christian relations, we might be tempted to downplay those aspects of Christian faith likely to provoke the most friction between Christians and Jews. But opting for inclusion over exclusion, rejecting the insider-outsider distinction, doesn't mean erasing difference. It means finding ways of building community with those who do not see or engage with the world the way we do. It means offering as well as accepting the challenge of difference. At the same time, it means recognizing that the Gospel is an antidote to strategies of exclusion, strategies that treat difference as an occasion for domination and subordination. The Gospel calls us, with the psalmist, to the unqualified praise of a God who is not the private property of any single community, but the God of all creation.

Part III
Identity and Community

18
What Makes Us What We Are?

Different strands of the Bible reflect contrasting responses to the problem of personal and corporate identity. Sometimes, we see what happens when, self-protectively, exclusivistically, we grasp our identities tightly and refuse to let go, no matter what. And sometimes we discern hints, or more, of another possibility—that of *affirming identity* without *rejecting difference*.

In Numbers, we are face to face with Israel at its most violent. Battling with the Amorite king Sihon, Israel takes "possession of his land from the Arnon to the Jabbok." Israelite spies explore Jazer, and Israel captures its villages and dispossesses the Amorites already in residence. And in conflict with Og, king of Bashan, the Israelites kill "him, his sons, and all his people, until there . . . [is] no survivor left; and . . . [occupy] his land." The interests of the invading Israelites are treated as if they take clear and unmistakable precedence over those of the Amorites and the people of Bashan. There is a great gulf fixed here between insiders and outsiders. The Israelite community asserts its identity forcefully and unequivocally in a way that excludes the claims of others.

Then, consider a story found in Luke's gospel: Jesus heals a crippled woman on the Sabbath, and this violation of traditional propriety offends the authorities: "There are six days," says the synagogue ruler, "on which work ought to be done; come on those days and be cured, and not on the Sabbath day."

The Sabbath was the distinctive sign of Jewish identity. In the wake of the Exile, which they attributed in part to their ancestors' disregard for the Sabbath, the Jews had hedged it about with restraints and prohibitions designed to ensure its proper observance. Proper Sabbath observance symbolized and guaranteed Israel's endurance as a unique community of faith. Keeping the Sabbath clearly demarcated the boundary between "us" and "them." While for *Jesus* the traditional way of keeping the Sabbath took second place to the health of the crippled woman, for his opponents her welfare seems to be significantly less important than the preservation of national identity.

Of course, those who confront Jesus in this story over his decision to heal the crippled woman may well be concerned, not simply that he has *healed on the Sabbath* but that *he* has healed on the Sabbath. Their reaction likely reflects their concern not only with Jesus' offense against the sanctity of the community's principal identity marker *but also* with his personal challenge to *their* identity as Israel's religious authorities.

The two issues are hard to separate. For the maintenance of a thriving community does require some measure of structure and stability. We do not need to understand the Jewish leaders' concern with their power in this story as consciously arrogant or self-interested—the exercise of their authority really *could* contribute to the continuation of the community's identity as they understood it. Once one takes oneself to be serving one's community in important ways, though, it becomes disturbingly easy to equate the interests of the community one serves with one's own interests. Preserving one's authority can appear deceptively to be, not a means of safeguarding one's own sense of value and one's material and social advantages, but a crucial ingredient in the protection of the group's shared life.

Probably, then, the Jewish leaders in this story respond to Jesus as they do because his behavior appears to threaten both their own identity as a class and that of the Jewish community as a whole. The people, however, do not appear to feel threatened. The "entire crowd," Luke tells us, "was rejoicing at all that wonderful things that he was doing." Just because power is used to preserve a community's identity does not mean that all the community's members will approve. Stable identities offer meaning and direction to persons and communities. But the felt need to preserve the security of a person or community's identity too often leads us to use power to exclude those in contrast to whom our identity is maintained and to corral those within our community whose behavior might upset its fragile order—and with it our identity as a group and our identities as individuals. This seems—in this story and those that follow it—to be the Jewish leaders' response to Jesus and those who acclaim him. If the crowd cheers Jesus on, the leaders apparently reason, they must be able either to *silence* the crowd or to *ignore* it, to define their community's character *unilaterally*. Otherwise, its identity will be lost—its identity, that is, as they conceive of it. The role of arbitrary power in maintaining identity is all too apparent when Jesus' opponents end forever on Golgotha, so they think, his threat to order and national identity.

Paul's behavior is in marked contrast with that of Jesus' opponents, and in likely continuity with that of Jesus. Throughout his career as an apostle, he confronted the challenge of simultaneously affirming his own, Jewish heritage while denying that Jewish identity and Christian identity were the same. His stance regarding circumcision, food offered to idols, and, perhaps (it's unclear), the Sabbath highlighted his position clearly: one did not need to accept a distinctively Jewish identity to join the Christian community.

This point needs to be stressed because it provides, I think, an important backdrop for the story of his discussion with Athenian thought-leaders on the Areopagus. Paul's argument in the first part of Romans parallels his approach to the presentation of the Christian message in Athens: he builds his case for Christianity on the basis of experiences shared by Christians and non-Christians. And yet many proponents of Christian exclusivism have alleged through the years that he judged his dialogue with the Athenian philosophers to be a failure. Reading too much into his claim that in Corinth he "resolved to know nothing . . . but Christ and him crucified," they have argued that at all costs Christians must affirm their distinctiveness, reject "worldly" wisdom, shun "worldly" people, hang on tight to their identity as a people—like those who slaughtered the Amorites, like those who condemned Jesus for violating the Sabbath.

But, in fact, Paul *nowhere* rejects the approach Acts depicts him as having adopted in Athens—and with good reason. It seems likely to have made sense, practically and theologically. Instead of damning the Athenians as heathen doomed to destruction, he argues that the God whose revelation he is announcing is actually the God whom they have worshipped "as unknown." He proclaims the infinity of God's being by citing a Greek poet. He enters into conversation with the intellectuals of Athens in terms they can understand. He doesn't shun them; he initiates respectful dialogue with them, articulating the good news in categories he shares with them. His awareness of these categories is evidence for an openness to Gentile culture that obviously preceded his arrival in Athens; a Roman citizen, he has not closed himself off to the non-Jewish world. And that he is willing to converse with the Athenians at all shows how different his stance is from a *militant* exclusivism disposed to justify the slaughter of those outside the Israelite community's boundaries, from a *haughty* exclusivism disposed to regard outsiders as unclean and contemptible.

Paul's concluding focus on Jesus' life beyond death makes clear that God's self-disclosure in Jesus remained his ultimate criterion for truth. The story of Jesus defined his identity and—we sense—he was proud of that fact. Though he rejected exclusivism, he was no relativist. Some, indeed, would argue that he was still too often narrow and arrogant. But he does seem to have affirmed that the God whose revelation is focused in Jesus is also the God known truly, if less clearly, in the ordinary world of human experience, to which he appealed in the Areopagus discourse and in Romans. As creator and redeemer, Paul was beginning to see, God is present *everywhere* to sustain, reveal, and deliver.

The difference between God and the world reduces to insignificance the differences that divide us from each other. At the same time, God is closer to us than those with whom we are united by bonds of identity. To worship the God revealed in creation, the God whose Word is "the light that enlightens everyone," is to move beyond exclusivism, to relativize our identities. It is to recognize that God does not inhabit a narrow district of history or experience, and that God calls us in Jesus to a reconciling love that inspires us to transcend our narrowness and exclusivity. The cross on which Jesus died—on which he died in part, we may suspect, because he threatened the security and stability of the Jewish community—is the end of the politics of exclusive identity, the ethics of exclusive identity, the spirituality of exclusive identity.

The point is not that community is wrong: we need to belong. We need connections, traditions, roots, identities. In a fragmented and unstable world, we need more bonds, more networks, more social support than we frequently experience. We need rich shared and individual stories that offer our lives meaning and purpose. But the example of Paul and the story of Jesus nudge us to recognize that no identity is or can be absolute. We need to take identity *seriously*, as an important constituent of our lives, but not *ultimately*, as the good that trumps all other goods. The appeal to identity can all too easily come to represent a deification of a community's current way of being and thinking and a silencing both of dissidents within and strangers without. At the personal level, appealing to identity can mean suppressing parts of oneself one would prefer to ignore or clinging to an imagined self—an anticipated or remembered one that does not really exist—rather than confronting the truth about who one is or could be.

A meaningful life—personal or communal—reflects an ongoing interplay of sameness and difference, continuity and rupture. Change and difference can be terrifying—threatening, we may feel, to destroy us. But the call to take identity seriously, but not ultimately, is a challenge to recognize that there may sometimes be things worse than the destruction of who we are at present. We need not *seek* disruptive, vertiginous change. We may, indeed, rightly *resist* it when it threatens values we hold dear. There may occasionally, though, come times when we must be willing to let go—when retaining our identity means holding on to injustice, untruthfulness, and exclusion, when change, by contrast, means openness to new possibilities of community and fulfillment we cannot afford to pass up. Letting go may mean a certain kind of death—the Jewish leaders saw that, and they killed Jesus rather than face it. But holding on *at such a time* means another kind of death, the slow dissipation of goodness and vitality that in the end robs life of ultimate worth. To recognize that identity is just one of the values we need to preserve in our individual and corporate lives, not the only one, is to welcome the future, God's future, and with it the surprising and ever-new gift that is God's grace, God's love, God's very self.

19
A Community of Love

The conviction that Israel was the special object of God's love nourished Jewish hope during centuries of conflict and uncertainty. But the genocidal massacres disturbingly depicted as accompanying the displacement of the Canaanites give bloody testimony to the potential destructiveness of believing that God cares for one nation more than for anyone else. Over time, however, God successfully wooed Israel toward a richer, more complex understanding of what it meant to be special. Israel could be special, not because it was the only nation God loved, but because it had a special gift to offer all people: an announcement and demonstration of God's all-embracing delight in and care for the whole of creation.

The experience of exile brought Israel and other nations into closer contact and challenged exclusivistic barriers. But it also threatened to destroy Israel entirely. In response, the nation became a fortress, with high walls designed to exclude not only military but also ethnocultural threats. Nehemiah broke up families and preached racial animus as he attempted to reconstruct Israel's identity. The Maccabees waged a guerrilla war against Greek occupying forces and against Jews open to Hellenistic culture to keep that identity intact. The residual feeling that being called by God meant being better than everyone else, and the understandable fears aroused by exile, bred a politics of Us and Them, a politics of purity, a politics of holiness.

Despite their other disagreements, major groups within Israel at the time of Jesus shared a commitment to the politics of holiness. Rigorous standards of behavior had to be followed to secure national identity—standards of diet, standards of worship, standards of friendship. Often, of course, adhering to those standards meant hating Rome, avoiding non-Jews, and rejecting those Jews who didn't measure up. Thus, a key reason for maintaining distinctive religious practices was to demarcate the boundaries between Jews and Gentiles, insiders and outsiders. Aliens were excluded from the temple, and purity was ensured by restricting women to a special temple court. The Pharisees boycotted agricultural products produced by non-observant Jews. Since poverty made payment of tithes and other religious duties impossible for many people, the poor were also stigmatized as unfaithful to God. Some people may have behaved like the father I read about some years ago who paid tithe rather than feed his family—and brought about the death of his son. Most, I'm sure, did not, and they were ostracized as a result. The Pharisees' boycott must have deepened the poverty of non-observant Jews. And to the extent that they shared the Pharisees' view of purity, people who were rejected by the faithful came to see themselves as unworthy and unloved by God.

Even, therefore, as a commitment to racial and cultural purity imperiled Israel's witness to God's universal love in Jesus' time, economic injustice also compromised its ability to affirm and embody that love. While tax collectors and other Roman agents and the members of the traditional upper classes prospered, peasants and other poor people chafed under the abuse of both their own people and the occupying authorities.

Jesus' contemporaries obviously had good reason to sing with the psalmist: "Turn not they servant away in anger, thou who hast been my hope. Cast me not off, forsake me not, O God of my salvation!" In Matthew, Jesus is characterized as God's response to such a call. The evangelist quotes the words of Isaiah that announce a new dawn for Israel and applies them to the ministry of Jesus. But it is interesting to note the immediately following words the evangelist does *not* quote: "For the yoke of his burden, and the staff for his shoulder, the rod of his oppressor, thou hast broken as on the day of Midian. For every boot of the tramping warrior in battle tumult and every garment rolled in blood will be burned as fuel for the fire."

Perhaps the evangelist does not quote words of vengeance because Jesus' ministry was not *about* vengeance. In place of the politics of holiness, Jesus offered a politics of hospitality. His ministry was not about vindicating Israel's claim to superiority. It was about reaffirming Israel's vocation as a community in which God's hospitable love was on display. Jesus rejected the emphasis on national purity that many of his contemporaries seemed to believe was necessary to keep Israel's identity intact. He rejected the rapacity of elites that kept peasants poor and marginal. He challenged the prejudice that stigmatized the sick as sinful, which is perhaps one reason Matthew's reference to Jesus' preaching the good news is followed immediately by the recollection that Jesus was known as a healer. Jesus' good news was the good news of hospitality, the good news that all of us are at home with God, and that God calls us to a common life in which that belonging finds tangible legal, economic, cultural, and interpersonal expression.

Jesus issued this call simply by being who he was: an infectious source of life and love. And he issued it by creating a small community that would serve as a laboratory demonstration of what was really good about the good news. Jesus didn't expect everyone in Israel to join his immediate entourage. But by calling the disciples, he brought into being a group with the potential to model what all Israel, and all the world, could be. God did not call Israel because of its spiritual superiority, but to challenge and empower it to embrace all creation. In the same way, Jesus called the disciples, not because they were better than everyone else, but so they could express in their shared life what God wanted Israel as a whole to be.

Building community has obvious advantages even for the selfish. Rejecting others breeds violence. Today's oppressed peasants may be tomorrow's revolutionaries. Jesus discerned what should have been obvious, that upholding national purity at all costs would get Israel nowhere. The Romans would tear down the walls of Jerusalem before they would allow Jewish nationalism to grow unchecked into successful rebellion. But crafting community and expressing love are not merely practical—they are the right things to do. Love and respect are ways we acknowledge the preciousness, the uniqueness, the irreplaceable worth of every person. Jesus called Israel toward a way of life marked by openness to the distinctive gifts of the strangers inside and outside its borders.

The gospel isn't about purity. It's about hospitality. It's about community. That's why the divisions that marked the Corinthian church distressed Paul so much. One reason that, as he says, "the word of the cross is folly" is that the cross displays not the power that dominates but the suffering love that embraces. Paul returns repeatedly in his letters to the message that boundaries that divide and marginalize have no place in the church. He is not always consistent, but he is at his most persuasive when he proclaims that all of us are one in Jesus. There are no barriers. There is just the hospitality, the inclusive love, of God. This is the gospel: the good news that God is with us and that, simultaneously, our loyalty to God relativizes all the loyalties, the identities, that keep us from extending hospitality to each other.

If we want to preach this gospel today in a way that is faithful to this crucial emphasis of Jesus' own preaching, and Paul's, we will need to look carefully at ourselves. When we practice rejection and exclusion in our personal lives, the gospel calls us to reach out in reconciling and accepting love. But we may find meeting some personal challenges easier than changing the tenor of our common life.

The poor still cry out as they did in Jesus' day for acceptance, for justice, for equal rights. They continue to be the victims of large-scale robbery and of privileges that keep them poor while benefiting the well connected at their expense. Legal and structural change may not do everything that needs doing, but they are essential elements of making the gospel real.

In too many churches, women can only be ordained to ministry by rogue congregations. In our culture, economic and emotional equality between women and men still elude us, men still earn significantly more on average than women, and intimates or ex-intimates will assault shocking numbers of women during their lives. People with dark skins or the wrong accents or the wrong papers or the wrong clothes or the wrong body shapes or the wrong sexual identities are still too often made thoroughly unwelcome. What will we, can we, do to display a gospel that rejects exclusion in the name of God's hospitality?

Christian faith is about the here and the now. It is about the difference God's love makes in the lives of people who cannot and should not escape from the reality of life in a hurting world. Jesus and Paul both make clear that the good news is the good news of loving community. They call us to announce that news today in ways that remake the fabric of our lives and the fabric of our world.

20
Jesus at the Party

Jesus liked parties. He seems to have been a popular guest—so popular, indeed, that some people who didn't like him called him a glutton and a drunkard. He clearly enjoyed the hospitality of his friends and acquaintances.

But Jesus wasn't just a guest: in another sense, he was also a host. He was inviting everyone to come home. He was calling Israel—and, though Israel, the world—to attend an incomparable party.

Offering food and drink is an especially powerful means and symbol of hospitality. So the psalmist depicts God as saying: "Open your mouth wide, and I will fill it. . . . I would feed you with the finest of the wheat, and with honey from the rock I would satisfy you." God's deliverance is represented by, and finds its fulfillment in, authentic hospitality, a rich banquet. Similarly, for Jeremiah, to be in right relation with God is to slake one's thirst, to drink from a bottomless well of cool water.

Hospitality is one of the greatest gifts we can offer each other. To feel welcomed in the warm and open space offered us by another is both liberating and empowering. It is when we know that we are at home that we can relax and display our true feelings. It is when we know that we are at home that can blossom, flourish, grow. The Gospel is the good news that we are at home in God. If we can truly grasp this truth—and it is anything but easy truly to make our own—we will understand that wherever else we may be at home, there is somewhere we belong.

Our own imperfect efforts to offer home to each other are sometimes profound sources of meaning and hope. It is sometimes, however, just when homes do best what we want them to do that they are distorted. For a home can all too easily become a fortress within which we hide from what is frighteningly different, disturbingly other than ourselves. Too often, we know who we are as family precisely in virtue of who is excluded from our acceptance.

The temptation is almost overwhelming to establish boundaries that exclude and reject those who are different. The challenge posed by difference is sometimes terrifying; it can make us dizzy. Responding to this challenge seems to have been near the top of Israel's agenda during the life of Jesus. Some people argued for a violent revolution that would evict outsiders from Israel. Others withdrew from ordinary life, building barriers between themselves and other Jews as well as non-Jews and foreseeing a day when divine vengeance would sweep away sin and sinners. Still others followed a meticulous path toward holiness within the day-to-day life of synagogue, market, and household, still very much aware of their difference from non-Jews and unobservant Jews. Others, of course, were happy to accommodate the Romans and to abandon many of the distinctive features of Jewish identity.

Jesus inserted himself into the ongoing debate about Jewish identity with a perspective that differed from all the other options on the table. Intensely aware of the presence and activity of Israel's God and the value of Israel's heritage, he did not share the accommodating conservatism of the Sadducees. At the same time, however, he resolutely opposed the rigid boundary definitions supported by other contemporary groups. An Israel intent on preserving its identity at all costs, an Israel determined to exclude outsiders, was an Israel destined for destruction. This wasn't because a vengeful God would impose some arbitrary punishment on Israel for the sin of exclusivism. It was because the inevitable result of exclusivism would be the confrontation with Rome that ultimately led to the destruction of Jerusalem four decades after Jesus was crucified.

Jesus believed passionately in hospitality, then, but not in a hospitality that was part of an unjust and self-destructive project. Calling Israel to a new kind of hospitality meant urging a new openness to the non-Jewish world. But it also meant encouraging a dissolution of the barriers within Israel.

In a rigidly structured society, where shame, honor, and social position are central preoccupations, hospitality can become a means of manipulation and a source of stressful obligation. The balance sheets must be kept in order: one favor demands another. Those on the upper rungs of the social ladder cement alliances with each other through hospitality while excluding others not as favored with wealth and status. By showing hospitality to each other, the members of the upper classes solidify their position and authority.

"Stop playing the status game!" Jesus almost shouts in response. "Stop worrying about repaying and being repaid." Jesus' startling injunction to his host undercuts the prevailing system of reciprocal obligations that kept the needy subservient and marginal.

Jesus wasn't issuing some sort of general prohibition of dinner invitations directed toward friends and relatives. Friends and neighbors celebrate with those who have found the lost sheep and the lost coin in Jesus' parables. And Luke includes in his Cornelius narrative in Acts a reference to the fact that the Roman centurion gathered "his kinsmen and close friends" to await Peter's arrival. Luke seems not to have seen a conflict between Jesus' injunction and the behavior of Cornelius or that of the figures in the parables. And of course Jesus himself seems to have been enjoying a traditional party as he spoke.

But it is important not to dull the edge of Jesus' point too much. Of course, our principal means of hospitality to "the poor, the maimed, the lame, the blind" are rooted in social cooperation, both the extended and often relatively impersonal cooperation of the market order and the deliberate, solidaristic cooperation of civil society. If we are to spread a rich banquet for the stranger today, we must do so as we structure laws, contribute to the shaping of culture, and help to define and support communal institutions. The lives of our communities—religious, civic, professional, affinity-focused—must all reflect a commitment to offering hospitality to those we do not know—those who differ from us in virtue of skin tone, accent, sexual orientation, or social class. Our first task, if we wish to show hospitality to strangers, will be in our schools, our businesses, in the editorial pages of our newspapers, on the streets of our cities.

But of course we cannot and will not welcome stranger into our public worlds while neglecting the strangers in our own private worlds. This will mean opening our congregations and our homes and our schools to the hungry and the homeless, the unemployed and the uneducated, the people who claim our attention and our care with the "Will work for food" signs they display at off ramps and intersections. It will mean giving of our money and our time and our emotional support to build relationships across boundaries of class and disability.

It is sometimes disturbingly easy to maintain a sense of moral and spiritual superiority when caring as we should for the economically vulnerable. But we may feel genuine discomfort when offering hospitality to other strangers. In reality, however, strangers of all varieties may be able to enrich our understanding of God, God's world, and our place in it. Each may have something of value to offer *us*. As we extend hospitality to strangers we may find ourselves welcomed and our worlds enlarged. The Catholic colleague, the Mormon student, the Buddhist girl who is dating your daughter: each of these strangers may have an angel's gift to offer if we will listen, if we will pay attention. But we must be ready to accept these gifts, to find them on offer in what we may regard as unlikely places.

God is our host for the richest of all banquets—the banquet of life. At this banquet, we, in turn, are called to host each other. God offers us a place called home. But that home is to be a home where all people are cherished and accepted, not an exclusive club to which the impure and unworthy are denied entry. Jesus' own ministry challenged his contemporaries, as it challenges us, to spread a banquet for all. As we do so, we help to make all people aware of what is, in any case, always true: that they are at home in God. At the same time, as we receive the gifts offered us by the strangers we welcome to our table, we learn in new ways what a glory it is to be at home with the God who invites us to the feast.

21
Dancing to the Flute

I got up in the middle of the night and sat, alone, in the family room. Like a number of those reading this book, I suspect, I was giving up my sleep so I could see Lady Diana Spencer marry the Prince of Wales. The beauty and youth of the bride, the splendor of the ceremony, and the wonder and excitement that so often accompany a wedding—with its new beginnings—combined to create a fairy-tale quality that caught the attention of viewers and commentators around the world.

There's something exciting about a wedding. Wearing "gold-woven robes," the bride in Psalm 45 proceeds toward hers with "joy and gladness." She and her husband can anticipate a future in which "all generations" and many nations will "praise [them] forever and ever."

When Rebecca's family sends her on her way with similar hopes that she will mother "thousands of myriads" of descendants, we understand: we understand her anticipation of the adventure she is beginning in a new land; and we understand her delight, and that of her family, at the prospect of an unending, legacy.

Jesus' hopeful joy mirrors that of these brides. He shares festive meals with his friends and sometimes his enemies, with the powerful and with the weak. He takes delight in the good things of the earth—good tastes, good scents, beautiful sights, warm friendships. But while people understand the celebration that surrounds a wedding, they don't seem so sure just what *Jesus* has to be so happy about. If Jesus is Israel's promised deliverer, why is he spending so much time going to parties? If he's speaking God's word to us, why is he hanging around with tax collectors and prostitutes? If he's calling us to repentance like John the Baptist did, how can he seemingly be enjoying himself so much?

Jesus observes wryly that his contemporaries didn't seem to have much use for John's asceticism, so it's a bit puzzling that they're unhappy with his enjoyment of the good things in life. What's wrong with a party, anyway?

In their different ways Jesus and John both unsettled and challenged their contemporaries. John bluntly confronted the evils in his society. Jesus' warm friendship challenged his contemporaries to break down the barriers that divided insiders from outsiders, the pure from the impure, so that everyone could come to the party, to the wedding, that was God's realm.

Maybe this all sounds harmless. But if Jesus was simply an apostle of niceness, the question naturally arises how he managed to get himself crucified. Receiving a party invitation doesn't orderly provoke the person receiving it to kill the one issuing the invitation.

The problem, I think, was the kind of party Jesus was hosting. Some parties seem to be fun, not so much because we want to see our fellow guests or spend quality time with our hosts, but because we've been invited when other haven't. We know we matter, we know we're superior, because we're on the inside and others aren't. Just belonging to an exclusive club—the one made up of the people lucky enough to get invited to *this* party—proves we're really important, really *special*.

At the time of Jesus, Israel needed reminders of its specialness. Its identity seemed threatened. After all, the Romans were in charge—and hostile to groups, like the Jews, who weren't prepared to assimilate. The Greeks before them had been determined to eradicate the distinctiveness of Jewish culture. And some Jews blamed compromise, a loss of some features of Israel's distinctive identity, for the exile and captivity that had devastated the nation centuries earlier. It was understandable that Jesus' contemporaries wanted to throw an exclusive party, a party at which they knew who they were because they knew who wasn't invited: the bad people, the impure people, the foreigners, the outsiders.

The kind of party Jesus was throwing was a different sort of party altogether. He challenged the view that excluding some people was the right way to make everyone else feel confident. He even predicted that an us-versus-them mentality would ultimately lead to a confrontation with Rome that would result in the destruction of Israel's holy city. Holiness didn't mean exclusivity, he suggested; it meant opening the nation's arms to embrace the rejected and the impure.

So we can see why many of Jesus' contemporaries didn't dance when he played the flute. There was reason to celebrate. He wanted them to experience the joy, the love, the communion—with God and with each other—that a wedding can symbolize and embody. But their sense of security depended on keeping some people at arms length, at enjoying communion with some while rejecting others. And that sense of security mattered more than the exhilaration and delight and liberation of new love that Jesus offered.

It's easy to look at Jesus' contemporaries with a sense of superiority. But don't we know something about rejecting outsiders? Intellectuals can look askance at those who haven't read the right books or don't speak in the proper idiom. Americans can rejoice smugly in American values, supporting international bullying and insensitivity by American politicians and refusing to learn from the experience of other societies and marginal social and political perspectives. Older people can condemn music, entertainment, and dress choices of younger people as vapid and superficial because they're unfamiliar—and in order to help them feel good about their superior insight and judgment. Men can exclude women's perspectives from considerations when they try to solve problems, reasoning that women are "too emotional" or "just silly."

Like the people who didn't dance when Jesus played the flute, we rely on rigid boundaries, on exclusion and rejection, more often than we'd like to think. Our passion to maintain our identities as persons and groups borders on the addictive. As we confront our addiction to being insiders, we will likely experience the kind of struggle Paul records in Romans 7. Paul's account is a classic depiction of idolatry that feels very much like a familiar modern narrative of addictive behavior. What seems good on one level doesn't seem to pack the emotional wallop of something I know is harmful and destructive. What we're addicted to seems to meet a profound need. We feel at some level that to let go of it would mean the end of us.

And of course in one sense it would. It would mean the end of a particular version of ourselves—stunted, cramped, cut off from reality, from others. And that can feel like death. Clearly, letting go of the insider-outsider system felt like death to many people in the Israel of Jesus' day. If God's realm was really a party like the one Jesus always seemed to be throwing, the things that told them who they were, that made them confident they were secure and loved, would have to go. They did what fearful people often, and understandably, do: they struck out.

We, too, may feel like striking out when the props that sustain our identities are challenged. Paul's experience as a Christian reminds us that there is no spiritual lobotomy that will free us in an instant from our addictions, including our addiction to the insider-outsider system. The gospel is a call, however, to move beyond this and other addictions, to see our communities and achievements, the good things in our lives that we rightly value, as *important* but not ultimate. It is a call to stop expecting these things to give us absolute security. And it is, in turn, an offer of real security, an offer of a real home, in God—an invitation to a wedding. We cannot expect an overnight reshuffling of our psyches. But we can and must begin to let go of our addictive idolatries. We can begin to let go of our heavy burdens. If we take Jesus' words as a striking clue to the inclusive, all-embracing love God offers us in place of our idols, we can begin to let God give us rest.

22
The Good News of Belonging

"How very good and pleasant it is when kindred live together in unity!" the psalmist exclaims. How good and pleasant it is indeed. Few things can hurt us more than conflict with the people to whom and with whom we belong. And few things are as powerful as being reconciled with people we love.

I don't have any siblings, but I still think it's easy to imagine the encounter between Joseph and his brothers as is portrayed in Genesis 45. This is the stuff of high drama: betrayed and sold into slavery by his brothers, Joseph now welcomes them with open arms. It's a profound story of forgiveness and hope. And it's understandable that Christians reading it have seen in it a foreshadowing of Jesus' forgiveness of his enemies—enemies who were and are at the same time sisters and brothers. The story of Joseph tells us that it is possible to move beyond the things that divide us—including the truly awful things we can do to each other. It says that reconciliation is possible, and that it brings joy and new life.

Joseph's story is a gospel story. For the gospel is the good news that we truly have a place we can call home. It is the good news that peace is more fundamental to human reality than conflict, community than enmity, belonging than alienation. Human beings all belong to and with God, so there is nothing to keep us all from belonging to and with each other. That is why, in the gospel story, Jesus embraces the Syro-Phoenician woman in a way that suggests the importance of transcending ethnic divisions. We are *all* God's chosen people.

The good news of belonging was at the heart of Paul's message. The divisions that separated Jew and Gentile had broken down and this fact constituted a profound religious revolution.

Paul's passion for community makes his reflections on the people Israel especially poignant. Paul the Jew, follower of Jesus the Jew, knows that there is a deep rift between Christians and the rest of Judaism. And so there's a problem. How can the gospel be the good news of community between Jew and Gentile if there is a profound rift between Jew and Gentile? If we are to trust in God's faithful love as the source of our belonging, can we say that God's covenant with Israel has changed? But if it has not, what can it mean if Israel does not see in Jesus the fulfillment of this covenant?

Throughout Romans 9-11, Paul wrestles, seemingly unsure how to understand the relationship between the people Israel and the emerging Christian community. Of one thing Paul is certain: God has not rejected Israel. Having given divine love to the Jewish people, God will not retract the gift. God's purpose is to "be merciful to all." Earlier, in Romans 5:18, Paul affirms that the good news means "justification and life for *all*." In 1 Cor. 15, he proclaims that "as all die in Adam, so *all* will b made alive in Christ." It is a central element of the gospel in the Pauline tradition that "all things, whether on earth or in heaven," have been reconciled to God, that "the grace of God has appeared, bringing salvation to *all*." Paul's own arguments are tortuous and sometimes troubling. But he is sure that God loves Israel and that, as he says in verse 25, "all Israel will be saved." Later Christians have not always related so positively to the people of Paul and Jesus. They have subjected Israel to everything from schoolyard taunts to confinement in ghettoes to pogroms to Hitler's Final Solution.

Christian rejection of the Jewish people is not simply an old-world problem. I remember my father talking about the pain of Jewish students he knew growing up in predominantly Catholic New England. In the years before the Supreme Court banished religious partiality from the public schools, it was still possible to hear Jewish students called "Christ-killers" and to watch them try to leave, quietly and unobtrusively, as Christian prayers were said and as Christian carols were sung at Christmas-time. And anyone who knows the history of American higher education will recall the ways in which, well in to this century, Ivy League colleges and universities limited the number of Jewish students they admitted.

We do not have to follow all the moves Paul makes in his efforts to make sense of Christianity's relationship with the Jewish people. We surely *must*, however, follow him in seeing that relationship within the setting of God's all-embracing love. If God intends the salvation of all Israel, we can be no less inclusive in our sympathies.

This does not mean, of course, that we should paper over our differences. Some Christians and some Jews may disagree about the nature of divine and human forgiveness. They may differ about the nature of our hope for the future and about what humanity's responsibility in history really is. Their views of what it means for humans to be God's covenant partners may not be the same. They may adopt varied views of the policies of the state of Israel and its treatment of the Palestinian people. But Christians cannot be true to the gospel if they fail to see the Jewish people as God's people, as their kindred in God's love.

The solution to the problem of our relationship with the Jewish people is thus as old and as simple as the gospel. The letter to the Ephesians maintains that the mystery of God's will is "to gather up *all* things . . . in heaven and . . . on earth." And "the mystery of Christ" is that "the Gentiles have become fellow heirs, members of the same body [with Israel], and sharers in the promise . . . ." Let the words sink in: *the end of division*, not some arcane celestial transaction, is the mystery of Christ. "[B]oth groups [have been made] into one and . . . the dividing wall, that is, the hostility between . . . [Jew and Gentile]" has been "broken down." The gospel says that we are all at home.

The gospel calls us, then, to meet the Jewish people like separated kindred, to greet them with outstretched arms. Christians may have been victims of Jewish hostility in the first century. Whatever the conflicts of that long-ago era, however, century after intervening century has provided Christians with more than adequate opportunities to turn the tables. Jesus and Paul sought to abolish the distinction between Jew and Gentile, but, ironically, subsequent Christians often restored it with a vengeance. So we must meet our Jewish kindred as Joseph's brothers are depicted as meeting him in Genesis—prepared to acknowledge our brokenness and the pain we have caused, and so prepared to accept forgiveness.

As it was first proclaimed, the gospel was centrally about community—and especially community between Jew and Gentile. We need to recover the good news of belonging today, and we need to begin by renewing our relations with the people Israel and with individual

Jewish people and congregations. Reconciliation doesn't mean an end to discussion—even heated discussion. It does mean experiencing the reality of God's inclusive love in our ordinary world today. When we make that love real in our relations with the Jewish people we will know more fully the joy of dwelling in unity with our kindred (who are ultimately, of course, all creatures). We will understand more deeply the revolutionary reconciliation that is the mystery of Christ.

23
Insiders and Outsiders

"You're fired." "God made Adam and Eve, not Adam and Steve." "Faculty members only." "Whites only." "Men only." "No Irish need apply." "I don't love you." There are few more painful words than those that tell us we do not belong: The feeling of exclusion gnaws at us, humiliates us, demeans us, angers us. So it may sometimes be easy for us to forget the impulses that lead others to exclude—and that lead us to do the same.

The conquest of Israel by Babylon, the exile of the Jewish people, and the occupation of Israel by foreign powers left a deep wound in Israel's psyche. Believing that the exile was a divine judgment on the nation's unfaithfulness, Jewish leaders urged a renewed commitment to the observance of Torah and an intensified emphasis on Jewish identity. The cultural—and, ideally, physical—boundaries between Israel and other nations should be firm and high, they believed. Maintaining a clear sense of *us* and *them* would simultaneously help Israel remain in right relationship with God, and so preserve the divine favor whose loss had led to the exile and occupation. At the same time, it would protect the nation against the encroachment of alien cultures. Non-Jewish culture was emphatically rejected, and non-Jews were marginalized—witness the mass divorces brutally mandated by Ezra.

The "politics of holiness" bred exclusion and subordination. But it grew out of a fear that Israel itself would be subordinated and its identity lost. Israel's leaders seem often to have believed that only if the nation were preserved intact, free from foreign influences, could it continue to enjoy God's blessing—and continue to perform the special work God had assigned to it. They remembered the exile with regret and experienced the Roman occupation with resentment.

Thus, by the time of Jesus, the "politics of holiness" played a vital role in Jewish life. Dominant voices suggested that those who were not scrupulous about ritual and purity were not good Jews; the Pharisees may even have boycotted their agricultural products. Jesus confronted this emphasis on boundaries throughout his ministry with a "politics of compassion." He gave voice to an inclusive vision of God's work in the world, one that embraced outsiders—not only women, children, and the poor but even non-Jews. The Fourth Gospel, which identifies him as the visible presence in the world of "the light that enlightens everyone" portrays him as declaring that, when crucified, he will draw *all* people to him—not just the insiders but *everyone*.

Jesus' injunction to love enemies will have been understood as a direct reference to Rome's occupying forces, one that called his contemporaries to reject the politics of *us* and *them*. The hearers of his parable of the "Good Samaritan" would have known that the Levite and the Pharisee observing the wounded traveler in his story would have suffered ritual defilement had they stopped to help the traveler. The Samaritan, an outsider, simply doesn't care about the laws of ritual purity—he provides the assistance the traveler needs. He does so, ironically, using oil and wine that were, because they were his, *also* impure—with the result that the wounded man would have been rendered impure by contact with them, and should, if he cared about purity, have refused the Samaritan's help. The parable registers a deliberate protest against the focus on purity that grew out of the "politics of holiness."

The ecstatic delight expressed in the psalms suggests one of several reasons for the final inadequacy of the politics of holiness. The psalmist does seem to think of Israel as "the people close to [God's] heart." The emphasis on God as creator points in another direction, however. The whole creaturely world is God's: the sky and the ocean; the angels; the sun, moon, and stars; sea creatures; natural phenomena; trees and animals—and "all nations" and "all rulers on earth." God is the God not just of one nation, one district, one region, one land, but of the whole world. Everything that *is* is God's good creation.

Despite the testimony to the universality of God's love offered by the idea of creation, by aspects of the biblical tradition like this psalm, and in Jesus' own teaching, it is obvious that Jesus' followers did not come immediately to share his concern to challenge the politics of holiness, and so to break down the barriers between insiders and outsiders. The story of first-century Christianity is arguably as much as anything a story of conflict between includers and excluders, people who see God's love as embracing everyone and those who see the maintenance of boundaries as crucial.

Though Paul suggests in Galatians that it took time for Peter adequately to grasp the implications of Jesus' commitment to a politics of inclusion, he stands tall in the story from Acts in which he ultimately rejects purity boundaries between Jew and Gentile. Despite his fear that his fellow believers might not understand, he had the courage of his convictions as he emphasized his reasons for violating traditional ritual purity taboos. The distinction between the circumcised and the uncircumcised, he maintains, simply doesn't matter. Whether because of the powerful dream of the net full of unclean animals which Acts describes him as having had, the evidence provided by the lives of non-Jewish Christians, or other factors, Peter seems ultimately to have been convinced that God loves, and seeks the love of, Jew and Gentile alike.

While the Apocalypse of John contains depictions of revenge, and though it sometimes seems anything but inclusive in its vision, its concluding passages are rich with images of community and peace that seem entirely consonant with Jesus' "politics of compassion." The seer depicts the arrival of a new cosmos, and with them the tangible presence of God. "Now," says the voice from the throne, "the dwelling of God is with people, and [God] will live with them. They will be [God's] people, and God . . . will be with them and be *their* God. [God] will wipe away every tear from their eyes."

The present age ends, for the Apocalypse, with the announcement that God will be with us. We do not need to struggle to secure divine favor by seeking purity, adhering to ritual laws, or practicing the politics of holiness: God will be *with us*, and who we are will be a function not of our success in preserving boundaries but rather of God's gracious love. And if God will be with us, then to be like God means that we can and should be with each other, not hiding behind the walls of purity and exclusion but as vulnerable as the God we meet in the one who exposed himself to a death John says would "draw all people" to him.

Unfortunately, when we affirm the value of inclusion, when we reject the politics of holiness, we may find it disturbingly easy to engage in our own brand of exclusion. Christians have often told the story of first-century Israel's concern with holiness in ways that have depicted Judaism as a corrupt tradition obsessed with behavior and unconcerned with the life of the spirit. But it would be a painful irony if a celebration of God's compassion led us to engage in rejection and marginalization ourselves. It is important to remember that the politics of holiness grew out of an understandable fear that Jewish identity would be lost. It is also important to remember that not all Jews at the time of Jesus would have sought to enforce norms of ritual purity in the same way as those whose views he opposed. It is crucial to recall that a concern with purity, exclusion, and boundary maintenance is not integral to Judaism—and that Jesus' goal was not to found a new religion but to defend a particular interpretation of what Judaism was and should be. It is worth emphasizing the wide range of positions that obtained within Judaism throughout its history. And, painfully, it must be stressed that Christianity has never been immune from the temptation to practice the politics of exclusion and identity-maintenance—not least by persecuting and oppressing Jews.

So challenging the politics of holiness must be about challenging ourselves rather than finding new excuses to exclude others. As we structure the institutions within which we work and worship and play, as we make a range of ordinary, day-to-day choices, we can opt to include or exclude, to tell people they belong or insinuate that they do not. Because God is the creator of us all, we can remember, with Peter, that God calls us to transcend the assumptions we often make about purity. We can recall with the Fourth Evangelist that God seeks to draw all people into a loving embrace. With the psalmist, we can celebrate all of creation as the theater where God's presence is evident and God's glory displayed. And we can begin even now to realize the world of compassion and inclusion that is prefigured in Revelation's proclamation of a God who makes all things new.

24
An Invitation to the Feast

I still recall the surprise, the awkwardness, the dismay with which I greeted the suggestion, during my first year in England as a graduate student, that I participate in in-person church fundraising efforts. I cringed at the thought of going door to door or pub to pub in search of money—and the opportunity to hand out literature about Christianity. I suspect I wasn't alone in my discomfort. For everyone who finds this a fruitful experience, there must be hundreds of people who find publicly representing the church in this way deeply unpleasant.

So many of us, though, grow up hearing the call to public evangelism. And we may hear this call in familiar Gospel passages. "From now on," Jesus says to the surprised Peter in Luke 5, "you will catch people," not fish. And along with James and John, Peter decides to follow the stranger who has entered his boat.

This isn't a call like the one Isaiah famously records, an epiphany in which the glory of God is unmistakably, overwhelmingly present. It is clear from the behavior of the disciples throughout the gospels that they lack anything like the unequivocal sense Isaiah seems to have of who God is and what God wants. They're puzzled. They're confused. Where Isaiah sees the brilliance and beauty of God, they contemplate an obscure present and an incomprehensible future.

Isaiah, it appears, believes himself called to carry a very specific divine message to Israel, a message of woe and destruction—and eventual hope. Here, too, there is a contrast with the disciples. There is no clear sense in Luke, or in the essentially parallel passages in Mark and Matthew, of what it means for them to "catch people." The call of the disciples comes after Jesus has begun his ministry of healing and preaching. God's activity is *breaking in* in a new and exciting way, he announces—as he challenges people to be part of what God is doing. And *then* he calls the disciples. As he has called them to participate in the divine project he embodies and is effectuating, they are to call others to do the same.

Unavoidably, we read this story through our twenty-first century lenses, in an environment in which public evangelism continues to be a staple of church activity. When we hear the disciples called to catch people, we think of the song so many of us learned an age ago: "I will make you fishers of men, fishers of men, fishers of men; I will make fishers of men if you'll only follow me." We read this as a story of disciples called to be missionaries, to be evangelists.

In a sense, we would be right. They are clearly missionaries: they are called to the quite specific mission of joining Jesus in the vanguard of God's inbreaking new order. And they are evangelists: they are to carry good news about what God is up to in Israel's history.

But, despite the confusion created by Matthew's pious substitution of "kingdom of heaven" for the doubtless more original "kingdom of God," Jesus' preaching wasn't designed, *per se*, to tell people how to, as we say, "go to heaven." He wasn't commissioning the disciples to help people "get right with God" individually, even though individual lives would doubtless be healed because of their ministry. He was giving them the chance, and giving them the chance to encourage others, to be part of the transformation of Israel as a community.

Jesus clearly cared about particular persons: think, for instance, of his tender care for the woman who anointed him with costly perfume, despite the disapproving titters of many of those who observed her action. He was recalled, particularly in the Fourth Gospel, as a person who deeply valued personal connections, intimate friendships. But the call of the disciples makes the most sense in light of an understanding of Jesus' ministry that highlights his commitment to a new kind of community in Israel.

Jesus' contemporaries faced a challenge: what kind of community would Israel be? Some believed that their nation could court divine favor in a way that would result in the expulsion of the Romans by emphasizing national purity. Rigid social boundaries would keep Jews from being polluted by contact with non-Jews, and observant Jews from being defiled by the impurity of non-observant ones. The holy people, the good people, would make the rules.

Some people thought those rules would be enforced by social pressure. Some thought the law would enforce them after the Romans had been evicted militarily. Some believed that Israel's only hope was the establishment of a community of the pure, the elect, far away from the corrupting influences of the Roman's and the Jewish establishment alike.

But Jesus, as far as we can tell, rejected all of these options. He, too, was concerned with the restoration, the transformation, of Israel. But he sought to create an Israel distinguished precisely by its rejection of the distinction between the pure and the impure, its openness to the putatively undesirable, its inclusiveness, its embodiment of God's grace. He wanted an Israel that was radically transformed, but not by a violent revolution in which the holy insiders expelled the impure outsiders. He wanted a new community, but one that embraced all Israel, and ultimately all the world, not one hidden away in an enclave of the pure by the Dead Sea. Like the psalmist, Jesus praised a God who rejected self-righteousness and cherished those marginalized because of their low positions. He anticipated the dramatic action of a God who would not abandon Israel and whose purposes would be mightily fulfilled. And he called the disciples to join him in achieving this God's purposes in the history of Israel.

Perhaps this offers us a useful perspective on the evangelistic task. The God of the gospel loves all people. The God of the gospel embraces and forgives and heals. The gospel would be anything but good news if it were the announcement that God can cherish and love those who respond correctly to our evangelistic efforts. But what if— as I suspect is true in the gospels themselves—evangelism isn't about ensuring that people accept the right beliefs and avoid evil behaviors so God can take them to heaven? What if evangelism is about something else entirely: about participating in God's work of crafting a new kind of human community? That might be something about which to get excited.

Consider the possibility of a community in which people who felt excluded everywhere else felt welcome. Consider the possibility of a community that put on display a style of life that challenged the penchant for hierarchy, rejection, and subordination that all of us confront in many of the environments in which we work and live.

Consider the possibility of a community in which purportedly "pure" people weren't warned away from the supposedly "impure," and in which the "impure" weren't encouraged to avoid polluting the orderly lives of the "pure." Consider the possibility of a community that fearlessly, buoyed by a hope beyond death like that to which Paul witnesses in 1 Corinthians 15, proclaims that it's OK to be offer and celebrate grace even in the face of the threats of torturers and tyrants.

We might participate in announcing the possibility of such a community—in both word and deed—in a variety of ways. We might still reflexively shun some of the difficulties associated with this kind of evangelism. But I believe we might find, in any case, that "catching people" for God's inclusive community might be something that, at least some times, we could actually find exciting.

25
On Being Prodigal

Most of us are not prodigals. Perhaps we should be. Perhaps there's something to be said for living with passion even when self-destructiveness is a by-product of our enthusiasm. But, in any case, we're not. Most of us surely resemble the uptight older brother in Jesus' story more than we do the wastrel who blows his inheritance partying and ends up working in a pig sty.

At least as it's framed in Luke's gospel, the story of the prodigal seems designed primarily to make a point to people who thought of themselves rather the way the older son did—people deeply skeptical about the inclusiveness of Jesus' vision of God.

Many first-century Jews must have struggled to understand their place in the world. Despite the belief that their ancestors had entered an everlasting covenant with God, it was hard to square the conviction that they were objects of special divine favor with the fact that they had been incorporated into the Roman Empire. Many of Jesus' contemporaries seem to have imagined that they could recapture God's good will by rigidifying the boundaries that separated them from other people, clearly marking the difference between the good and the bad—and firmly excluding the bad. And "the bad" here included not only non-Jews but also those Jews who didn't measure up, in various ways—because, say, they were unconcerned about purity rules, or were overly friendly with foreigners.

Jesus, too, was interested in Israel's identity as a covenant community. But he seems to have thought that the way to enliven the community was not to make it more exclusive but rather to make it more inclusive. He painted a picture of a God whose arms were open to the world, and he called his contemporaries to exhibit a similar openness.

Not surprisingly, his conception of a God whose embrace was as wide as all creation made some people uncomfortable. Being able to clearly to identify insiders and outsiders tells us who we are—we're the insiders, of course—and we don't like the thought of losing our place at the table.

This kind of tendency is especially common among those who are oppressed, as first-century Jews surely were. Appeals to shared identity can often serve to inspire people to stand firm in the face of authoritarian rule, to resist subjection to tyrants. And it can be easy to hang on to a way of being in the world that makes coping easier, that helps to keep the hope of liberation alive. Unfortunately, the seeming value of clinging to a sense of who we are in contrast to them can obscure the fact that, even if we're trying to resist oppression, owning ourselves as insiders while rejecting others as outsiders can turn us into oppressors. Unfortunately, it's perfectly possible to be on the receiving end and the giving end of oppression at the same time.

I was about to sum all this up by saying that Jesus' contemporaries resisted his inclusive message. But of course that wouldn't be quite right. Jesus' contemporaries, like people everywhere, were diverse and complicated. Different people had their own perspectives and concerns and commitments. Some people resisted what Jesus had to say: those who exercised power and understood themselves as the guardians of the *status quo* or as the protectors of Israel's specialness.

Other people, including, one suspects, many ordinary people, had little investment in the idea that distinguishing Jews from gentiles and good Jews from bad Jews was the path to a better life. Certainly, many people seem to have welcomed what Jesus had to say. But the gospels give us reason to think that influential people who felt threatened, in various ways, by what Jesus had to say did, indeed, challenge him at every turn.

On Luke's view, that's why Jesus told this story. While the prodigal son gets the most overt attention, and while the love of the waiting father is surely the most important take-away from the story, Jesus is obviously very concerned with the reactions of his critics. The prodigal son is the paradigmatic bad Jew: he tells his father, in effect, that he doesn't care if he's dead, and, after he has wastefully exhausted his inheritance, he is rendered profoundly unclean by his association with pigs. But his father, perhaps suppressing his own instincts at more than one point, welcomes him home with warm and loving arms—arms that, as in today's psalm, offer protection from trouble, surrounding a beloved child with songs of deliverance.

If a human father can behave this way—and who wouldn't regard such a father as exemplary?—then surely God can do so. We can hardly expect less of God than we expect of ourselves. And if God can behave this way, shouldn't those who seek to be God's ambassadors do the same?

While Paul envisions *the church* as a divine embassy, Israel had long understood itself to have a vocation to serve as "a light to the nations." But a fearful, constricted understanding of that vocation led too many people, responding to what they saw as Israel's abandonment by God, to seek to realize it simply by being pure, holy, in ways that would earn God's renewed affection. Jesus, by contrast, proclaimed the message of a universally welcoming God and urged his contemporaries to fulfill their vocation precisely by emulating that God.

It's naïve to suppose that Jesus was ultimately executed because he thought, and proclaimed, that God was nice. Proponents of niceness are patted on the back approvingly, or else simply ignored. It is very difficult to sort out what happened in Palestine almost 2,000 years ago, but what is clear is that what Jesus said and did proved intensely threatening to people with power. For the Romans who actually carried out the execution, predictably alert to the possibility of insurrection, the simple fact that Jesus was charismatic and that a great many people followed him enthusiastically may have been enough. The socially and religiously and politically prominent Jews who opposed him may have felt, at some deep level, that who they were and everything they were trying to do was threatened by the message of an open, inclusive covenant. As today's passage from Joshua reminds us, their ancestors had eaten "the produce of Canaan," taken at sword's point from people whose cities were burned, whose land was stolen in the name of God. But what if God proved not to be the God of xenophobic violence, of religiously legitimated thuggery? What if God was the God of peaceful, voluntary cooperation? Perhaps the whole project in which they were invested was deeply problematic. Perhaps the kind of community they hoped to create or recreate wasn't the kind of community God was actually seeking to establish. Perhaps their power was suspect, their positions unwarranted, their purity pointless. Perhaps if people understood Jesus' message, their influence would evaporate and their goals for Israel prove unachievable.

So much speculation; so little certainty. What we do know is that people care about being right and about excluding or subordinating those they take to be wrong. We know that good people, people like the older brother in Jesus' parable, people like us, sometimes do the worst things in the name of righteousness, using power to obliterate what doesn't fit, those who don't fit. We know, too, that to confess that God is love is to name God as One who embraces us even when we reject and dominate in the name of righteousness—but also that to make this sort of confession is to open ourselves to being ambassadors for a God of grace who wants us to craft a community today, in this place, in which all are welcomed and embraced.

26
A House for God

David wants to build a house for God. Other local deities had houses, after all. And David is grateful to God for bringing him to the throne, for helping him to overcome adversity and establish and large and peaceful kingdom.

But the prophet Nathan says to him, clearly, that God does not need or ask for a house. Indeed, instead of demanding a house from David, God will build a house *for* David. David's son—who will build the temple God does not wish David to construct—will be followed by a kingly line that will last forever.

As in 2 Samuel, so in Psalm 89, God's faithfulness is underscored. If David's children are disloyal to God, says the psalmist, seeking to speak on God's behalf, "I will not remove from him my steadfast love, or be false to my faithfulness. I will not violate my covenant, or alter the word that forth from my lips." No, says the psalmist, God's faithfulness will ensure that David's "line shall endure for ever."

The Gospels, particularly Matthew, present Jesus as the inheritor of David's title. And the reign of God he announces is to be seen, for the evangelists, as the continuation of the Davidic kingdom in a new and surprising form.

But where Psalm 89 focuses on David's heir as violently crushing enemies, Mark 6 depicts Jesus as a compassionate shepherd—an unexpected kind of king, one who rules through nurture rather than intimidation.

As the gospels recast the image of the Davidic king, so, too, do they, and the epistles, recast the idea of the realm over which the Davidic king presides. Declining to surround himself with the powerful, to participate in the games of power politics—of revolution *against* the Romans or appeasement *of* the Romans—Jesus began to create what Dom Crossan has called "a kingdom of nobodies."

The Israel of Jesus' day was a deeply divided society. There were substantial divisions of wealth and power. But, more than that, there were divisions related to the understanding of the nation's identity. Even though Israel had returned from exile in Babylon, the deep-seated fear persisted that the surrounding world wanted to destroy Israel as a community with a distinctive relationship with God. The depredations of Antiochus Epiphanes, who had sought to end Jewish worship and annihilate Jewish religious identity, had added to this fear, as had Rome's take-over of the nation.

Now, the question on the minds of thought-leaders and ordinary people was, "What does it mean to seek the renewal of Israel in this dark time of foreign occupation and apparent abandonment by God?" For the Sadducees, the answer seems to have been: *accommodation with Rome is the best way to preserve Israel and avoid a devastating foreign attack*. All of the other major social forces shared the view that purity was crucial to renewing Israel and keeping it in right relation to God. Outside cultures needed to be kept at bay, beyond protective cultural boundaries. And social barriers needed to keep the impure elements of Israeli society—people who didn't live up to the demands of religious law, perhaps because they were poor or had suffered some social disgrace—in their proper place.

For the Qumran community, the answer was: *good Jews should leave the mainstream of Israeli society and create a community apart, in which true holiness can be practiced, and which God will vindicate (whether through human or divine violence) in a final, apocalyptic war*. The so-called "zealots" sharpened their swords in preparation for acts of revolutionary violence against the Romans. And the Pharisees sought to live lives of responsible integrity and faithfulness in society in order to preserve Israel's covenant with God and guarantee divine favor.

Unavoidably, Jesus inserted himself into this debate. It is in relation to this discussion among first-century Jews about what Israel was and should be—about identity politics, if you will—that Jesus' words and deeds must be understood, rather than as concerned with the topics of later debates about faith and works and other questions.

What is striking about Jesus' intervention into identity politics is that he seems to reject the focus on purity, on boundary-maintenance, that preoccupied his contemporaries. Rather, his understanding of God's reign, his new vision of the Davidic kingdom, was of an inclusive community. Like Solomon before him, this son of David worked to build God a temple—a community constructed out of diverse materials. As Solomon brought gifts from those outside his country into the temple he erected, so Jesus attempted to build a community in which those who were not part of the country's mainstream—women, poor people, Roman collaborators, the ritually unclean, non-Jews—could be welcomed and accepted.

His proposal for the identity of his nation was radical. Instead of finding ways to shore up and protect the nation's existing identity against foreign incursions, might that identity itself be recast in such a way that welcome for the outsider, openness to the stranger, became its identifying mark?

That sense of what the new temple, the new "kingdom," might look like comes powerfully to expression in Ephesians 2. Here, there is the sense of a community in which "the dividing wall of hostility" between Jew and non-Jew has been razed, and peace has been made. This is not, as in later Christianity, a rejection of Judaism, but rather an incorporation of Jew and non-Jew alike in a shared "commonwealth"—understood as a community that is distinctive precisely because of its inclusiveness.

The message of "peace to you who were far off and peace to those who were near" is as powerful and profound and important a message today as it was when Ephesians was written and Jesus preached. That message of peace matters in a world in which rulers still seek divine authorization to crush their foes and strike down those who hate them. Especially in a time of international turmoil, may our community of faith, linking people in many lands and of many ethnic backgrounds, prove a safe and welcoming space in which people are united despite their differences, a community crafted into a new temple, "a dwelling place of God in the Spirit."

27
Mattering

For Isaiah and the psalmist, Israel is uniquely beloved by God, the object of distinctive divine regard. It is cherished and nurtured. And while the Letter to the Hebrews tells the hero tales of Chapter 13 as pointing toward the coming of Jesus, they still serve to remind those who read and listen to them of great moments in the history of a people claiming a special relationship with God. Where others might simply tell of battles and strong warriors and treasure, the hero tales to which Hebrews alludes depict the heroics of faithfulness, and so emphasize the centrality to Israel's self-understanding of its relationship with God, and thus, implicitly, its sense of its own distinctiveness.

But Israel is also capable of profoundly disappointing lapses. The psalmist calls on God to restore the fortunes of the nation. And for Isaiah, too, the once beautiful vineyard that is Israel has been laid waste, clearly by God. Isaiah says that God "looked for justice, but saw bloodshed; for righteousness, but heard cries of distress."

I want to suggest that we can see a link between the initial depictions Isaiah and the psalmist offer of national specialness and the injustice and collapse that follow.

Mattering *matters*. It is obviously among the chief delights of close friendship and romantic love that we know ourselves set apart

Human beings are necessarily finite. For me to set a friend or a lover apart is an unavoidable aspect of what it means for me to experience friendship or love: as an individual, I can only be close to you, I can only weave my identity and my life together with yours, by excluding. I am limited, finite; even if I wanted to be, I cannot be close to everyone. So my setting you apart is really no cosmic claim about your inherent superiority to everyone else; it is a reflection of a very human choice on my part—simply a choice, one occasioned by my finitude.

But, of course, God is, by definition, not finite. God can be close to all creatures. God can incorporate all creatures into the divine life, the divine identity, in a sense into the divine body—loving each one in passionate particularity without cherishing any other any less.

God can do this. And so the belief that God instead does something else could be a heady intoxicant indeed. For supposing that God, who could embrace all without preferring any, has chosen me and mine might well lead to the tempting belief that God's choice has signaled or established some kind of objective superiority: there's something about our performance or our task that makes us superior to others. And it is a sense of objective superiority that often lies at the root of injustice, bloodshed, and distress.

I hope it is clear that I don't think we should focus on ancient Israel in order to single out this community for more searching scrutiny than our own or any other. The sense that a particular historical community is God's chosen because it is somehow better than the others, or because God is committed to preserving it no matter what, is dangerous wherever it is found. Those who believe they are doing God's work—and why not think this, if one is God's chosen?—may be capable of anything.

Centuries ago, the great John Donne railed against, as he said, "the abomination of torture":

> They therefore oppose God in his purpose of dignifying the body of man, first who violate, and mangle this body, which is the organ in which God breathes, and they also which pollute and defile this body, in which Christ Jesus is apparelled; and they likewise who prophane this body, which is the Holy Ghost, and the high Priest, inhabits, and consecrates.
>
> Transgressors that put God's organ out of tune, that discompose and tear the body of man with violence, are those inhuman persecutors who with racks and tortures and prisons and fires and exquisite inquisitions throw down the bodies of the true God's servants to the idolatrous worship of their imaginary gods, that torture men into Hell and carry them through the inquisition into damnation.

Donne is all too right. And nothing, it may seem, has changed. In Donne's England, torture served the purpose of ensuring that Catholics would not impede the nation's achievement of its religious mission. Today, I fear, some people seem to support torture by the

US government in part because of a sense of America's place in God's project in the world and of Americans' putative moral superiority.

Perhaps the sense that specialness of the wrong sort can be destructive lies behind some of Jesus' words. He intends, it appears, to shatter the sense of communal solidarity—of insider identity, of *our* superiority over *them*—that can come too readily from a perception of one's own community as objectively special, as the supreme object of divine regard.

I don't myself believe that we can or must abandon the idea of election, of specialness. Individually, we elect others as objects of our love, discerning their uniqueness and making them special through our love. Divine election, in turn, can be recast as an awareness of the realities of history. The vicissitudes of our collective stories are such that some communities acquire insights and opportunities others lack. This is not because God's providence arbitrarily selects some and abandons others. It is because divine providential action itself occurs in and through the contingent, unpredictable processes of history, effected through and constrained by the choices of free creatures and the organic spontaneity of natural processes. If God's action in the world is persuasive, rather than coercive, no divine guarantee will ensure that everyone gains the same kind of understanding. There will be no way to ensure that the same truths will be on offer everywhere or that each community will have the same capacity to influence history for God.

But if a given community is graced with unique insights and opportunities, this will not be because God has arbitrarily elected it, or rewarded it for its virtue. It will simply be a matter of historical contingency, of which God's providence seeks to take effective advantage. And it will provide no reason at all to suppose that other communities lack valuable insights and opportunities or that a community that seems to have benefited especially from the circumstances of history will continue to do so consistently.

It seems to me, then, that we need to find ways of understanding historical distinctiveness as a source of gratitude and responsibility rather than arrogance. Recognizing the contingency of our circumstances can keep us from indulging in the arrogant supposition that our virtue or our achievement merit special divine favor. Though they might not share our contemporary sense of the radical contingency of history, the prophets would surely agree that the only kind of election worth affirming goes hand in hand with humility. And they would recognize, too, as did Jesus, that the failure to move beyond a sense of national superiority, to abandon a way of looking at the world structured around the celebration of one's own identity as superior and the exclusion of outsiders, can have devastating consequences. Jesus saw, I think, that it would lead his own people to a destructive and near-fatal confrontation with Rome; this may be part of what he had in mind when he talked about the importance of discerning the signs of the times. His words, and those of the prophets, remind us that the challenge to discern those signs is no less pressing today.

28
Encouraging Community

Therefore, *encourage*: that's the bottom line of Paul's injunction to the Thessalonians. Encourage one another and build one another up.

What's the therefore? "For God did not appoint us to suffer wrath but to receive salvation through our Lord Jesus Christ. He died for us so that, whether we are awake or asleep, we may live together with him."

You might think, at first glance, that this is a passage about life after death. Listening to a lot of modern Christian preaching—just flip across your radio dial if you don't know what I mean—might give you the impression that Christianity is about pursuing heaven and avoiding hell. Now, I don't want to pretend that there's no link between that kind of preaching and what Paul writes to the Thessalonians, but I suspect that Paul's thinking about this may be a bit more complicated than that of the radio preachers.

I think this because of verse 10: "He died for us so that whether we are awake or asleep, we may live together with him." Now, perhaps Paul means something like, "He died for us, so that, after the resurrection or in death, we may live together with him." Maybe that's right. But there's no reason to think Paul is talking about life after death in this particular sentence.

We may live with him while we are awake—that is, right now: that doesn't sound like Paul's talking about pie in the sky by and by when you die (in the words of the old folk song).

So I think it's fair to say that Paul is urging the Thessalonians, certainly, to encourage each other because they have hope in the future. But it's hard not to catch a hint, too, of the view that the Christians to whom he's writing ought to be encouraged because of Christ's presence with him in the present.

Now, look around. We don't see the human figure of Jesus, or hear his voice, or feel his hands on ours. I hope it will come as no surprise to you that Paul was aware of this. Some of what he writes suggests he himself had quite intense private mystical experiences. But there's no sense that he treated these as the norm. He didn't think that others would necessarily have similar experiences.

And I don't think he had in mind some kind of spiritual elitism: he wasn't saying, in effect: well, I've had these experiences, so I know you can be with Jesus right now; just trust in my experience. He certainly wants to be trusted, and he certainly thinks his experience has value. But he's not announcing dogmatically that the Thessalonians should live at one remove from his own, authentic experience, that their experience should be second-hand.

So, what does Paul mean when he says that we, who are awake, can live together with Christ? We begin to get an idea, I think, if we reflect on the repeated sense we get in Paul that Christians' experience of the Holy Spirit is their experience of the risen Christ. Consider the most striking of these passages, 2 Cor. 3:18: "And we, who with unveiled faces all reflect the Lord's glory, are being transformed into his likeness with ever-increasing glory, which comes from the Lord, who is the Spirit." Note that: "the Lord, who is the Spirit." There's a lot to be said about that, but I want to suggest, more than argue, just now that, when Paul talks about our living together with Christ while we're awake, right now, he's talking about our living in Christ's Spirit. I suspect he means that the early Christians' experiences of the Holy Spirit are experiences of Christ's presence: if the Holy Spirit is present and active in their congregations, then, indeed, they live together with Christ.

But this may just seem to push the problem back a step. For what did Paul mean when talking about the presence and activity of the Holy Spirit? Again, Paul himself was not opposed the idea that people can and do have intense and uncanny experiences that might disclose God in important ways. Still, I am reasonably confident that Paul isn't saying to the Thessalonians that they can be sure of God's presence in their midst because of some sort of peculiar, tingling sensation, or anything of the sort.

Instead, I suspect Paul thinks that the early Christians know the presence of Christ at least in part through the Spirit's gifts. For Paul, these gifts clearly include the remarkable—healings and deeds of power—as well as the more ordinary—teaching, for instance.

I don't think Paul would have been inclined to interpret these phenomena as evidence of Christ's presence had Jesus himself not done and undergone dramatic things, and had Paul himself not understood himself to have encountered Jesus alive after his death on the cross. I think he wants to make sense of what he and the other early Christians are experiencing and doing in light of Jesus' story. But, given that story, he wants to point to the tangible evidence of the Spirit's work as a clear confirmation that his congregants can, indeed, know themselves to be living with the risen Christ, even while awake, in the present.

What are we to make of this today? Some people report truly dramatic experiences that seem to violate our expectations about an orderly world in which ordinary creaturely events cause and are caused by other creaturely events. Reports of such events, if substantiated, could certainly serve as pointers to a world beyond our senses, and to the intersection of that world with our own. But that's not true for all of us, of course. It's not true, indeed, for most of us.

And it's hard to think of our experiences of ordinary gifts—teaching and preaching and serving—as independent evidence of God's presence and activity. We can certainly read our ordinary experiences as experiences of God in light of a warranted understanding of the world as God's creation and as a theatre of divine activity. But that understanding will be credible to the extent that it is at least consistent with, and, ideally, illuminative of our experience.

This passage in 1 Thessalonians doesn't seek directly to solve that problem. Paul assumes that his readers know themselves to be God's creatures and recipients of God's grace in Christ: his goal is simply to remind them of that. In light of the story of Jesus they already know, he underscores the fact that they can live together with Christ.

I suggest that reading our experience as experience of God is not a matter, at least not ordinarily, of looking for the dramatic and the miraculous, even if this would have been a part of what the early Christians would have seen as confirming the reality of God's presence with them. It's a matter of looking at the big picture: of finding belief in God and God's work in Jesus a source of illumination, coherence, and connection in our experience, and coming to interpret our experience in light of that story.

A crucial consequence of doing this, it seems to me, will be fostering a flourishing common life. Note that this is the focus of a tremendous amount of Paul's attention. Both in Chapter 4 and in the portion of Chapter 5 that follows it, Paul is concerned in very concrete terms with how the Thessalonians treat each other: "encourage the timid, help the weak, be patient with everyone. Make sure that nobody pays back wrong for wrong, but always try to be kind to each other and to everyone else."

God's presence among us couldn't be *constituted* by a flourishing community. We can't *make* God be present by treating each other better. Christians confess that God is *always* present and active *everywhere*. But living in light of God's grace-ful presence has to mean, at least, that we seek to live well with each other, too.

29
All Nations Stream to the Mountain

As with the coming of Jesus into the history of Israel, so with the future: we do not know what to expect, or when to expect it.

> No one knows about that day or hour, not even the angels in heaven, nor the Son, but only the Father. As it was in the days of Noah, so it will be at the coming of the Son of Man. For in the days before the flood, people were eating and drinking, marrying and giving in marriage, up to the day Noah entered the ark; and they knew nothing about what would happen until the flood came and took them all away. That is how it will be at the coming of the Son of Man. Two men will be in the field; one will be taken and the other left. Two women will be grinding with a hand mill; one will be taken and the other left.
>
> Therefore keep watch, because you do not know on what day your Lord will come. But understand this: If the owner of the house had known at what time of night the thief was coming, he would have kept watch and would not have let his house be broken into. So you also must be ready, because the Son of Man will come at an hour when you do not expect him.

At the same time, with Paul, we must recognize that we can discern the signs of the times. Thus, that for which we hope may become an inspiration for our work in the present.

First, we may seek a community that is inclusive. In Isaiah's vision of the last days, "all nations will stream" to the mountain of the Lord's temple. Too often, we opt for an understanding of our place in the world in which our community, our nation, our ideology reigns supreme, with others left on the outside, wailing and gnashing their teeth. In Isaiah's vision, by contrast, the temple becomes a home for all nations.

To be sure, Isaiah envisions all nations asking to be taught the ways of Israel. One the one hand, we do well to avoid the facile assumption that we do not have insights worth sharing, that we have nothing to teach others. On the other hand, the humility that prompts our recognition that we do not know the shape of God's final future should also prompt us to avoid any sort of smug response to the picture Isaiah paints, any dubious judgment that we and only we have the truth, and that only we have something to give, while the place of others is to receive. We must pray for the peace of our own city, with the psalmist, but we must not assume that only our city is worth praying for.

Instead, we must celebrate our opportunities to give what we know and cherish to others while recognizing that the coming of "all nations" to Israel provides not only the opportunity for Israel to give to the nations, but for the nations to give to Israel as well. We have something to gain, something to learn, from all those who inhabit God's world.

Naturally linked with inclusion is the call to peace in Isaiah's vision. Swords will be converted into plowshares, spears into pruning hooks. Nations will not go to war.

What a powerful image of the future this is, and how dramatically different from the world we inhabit. It is, of course, a logical concomitant of Isaiah's vision of inclusion. For the inclusive Gospel challenges us to see the other as a potential friend, not as an enemy. If that for which we hope becomes that for which we work, then we must recognize that peace must be our goal now, too.

I am not a pacifist. I believe that it is somtimes just to use force to prevent, end, or remedy aggressive attacks on bodies and justly acquired possessions. But I believe we can find it far, far too easy to opt for force as a solution to the challenges we face. In our personal lives, we may choose aggression and criticism over reconciliation. Institutionally, in church or institution, we may seek to steamroll those who disagree with us. Internationally, we may opt to resolve disputes using violence when diplomacy and economic pressure might be entirely satisfactory. If our vision of the future is, as in Isaiah, a vision of peace, we must ask what we might do to foster relationships—personally, locally, nationally, internationally—in which reconciliation happens, in which violence is averted, in which we seek to make war no more.

30
Heaven on Earth

After the arrest of John the Baptist, Jesus moved to Capernaum, thus, on the First Evangelist's view, fulfilling Isaiah's prophecy that divine light would dawn "on the road by the sea." He called his first disciples, and he began to preach: "Repent, for the reign of heaven has come near."

For a devout Jew of Jesus' time, speaking of "heaven" was a roundabout, respectful way of referring to God. When Jesus announced that the reign of heaven had come near, he wasn't trying to turn people's minds toward a place in which it's possible to be with God after death. Instead, he was proclaiming that God was up to something, up to something exciting.

Whatever the original provenance of Psalm 27, its words would surely have been meaningful to Jesus' contemporaries. The desire to live in God's house, to behold God's beauty, to be hidden by God's grace during a time of trouble—to be delivered: this desire was powerfully felt indeed in the Israel of Jesus' time. And Isaiah's declaration that God's light would dawn when the yoke of oppression had been broken would have resonated with his contemporaries, too. Devastated by centuries of invasion, occupation, and exile, Jews of Jesus' day yearned for restoration—for liberation from foreign domination, for renewed evidence of God's favor.

Many first-century Jews reacted to the threat of foreign oppression by emphasizing the need to maintain their nation's identity at all costs, to shore up the boundaries that separated Jews from non-Jews and good Jews from bad Jews, perhaps even to retreat from the ordinary social world into a secluded community of the pure. And they anticipated a future in which Romans and other foreigners would be violently crushed—perhaps by miraculous divine intervention, or perhaps by God's providential work through the people Israel (or a vanguard of revolutionaries).

In this context, Jesus' announcement of the imminent reign of God might initially have been heard as a prophecy of forthcoming violent revolt against Rome, and perhaps also against oppressive forces within Israel. But it is clear that, while Jesus stood passionately against Roman and Jewish oppression alike, he did not envision the future in the same way as did many of his contemporaries.

Jesus' call to *repent* would not, for his hearers, have been primarily a challenge to abandon personal sin or rely on divine grace in the hope of life beyond death. It would have meant to do what was needed for Israel to be restored. Ironically, this is likely to have meant, among other things, precisely the relinquishment of alternative popular strategies for Jewish renewal. These strategies seem, for Jesus, to have inhibited Israel's restoration rather than furthering it. Israel's leaders would need to give up the hope of violently confronting and expelling the Romans and their clients. They would need to stop trying to secure divine favor by guarding the boundaries between Israel and other communities and between insiders and outsiders within their nation.

Repentance was a matter of national transformation. So Jesus' call had concrete consequences for Israel's common life. It meant a new attitude on the part of particular people toward outsiders—Jews, gentiles, women, poor people, even people who collaborated with Rome and its client, Herod. It meant the transformation of Israel into a new kind of community. And it meant a confrontation at the center of religious, social, political, and cultural power, Jerusalem, where leaders continued to underwrite what Jesus clearly saw as a failed, self-destructive program of attempted national renewal. Jesus evidently shared his contemporaries' conviction that God cherished Jerusalem. But he also believed that the city's destruction was imminent—not because some miraculous divine judgment would topple its walls, but because Roman siege engines would do so if his people did not abandon their rejection of outsiders and their commitment to violence.

Jesus' confrontation with Israel's leaders in Jerusalem led, as we know, to his death. But his encounters with his followers after his death unleashed a powerful new dynamic in history. The creation of a new community, embracing Jew and Gentile alike, continued. A turning point had come in Israel's history, and through Jesus, his followers believed, Israel's God had communicated the truth that the divine love extended to those beyond the land's borders.

Once recognized as a God of universal love, God must be supposed always to have cared for and worked within all communities. But Jesus' ministry and its aftermath opened up the possibility of a new kind of community that transcended ethnic and cultural boundaries, in which all were united in the embrace of the one God.

So we can see one reason, immediately, why Paul finds the kinds of divisions he has heard afflict the Corinthian congregation so problematic. The message of the gospel is a message of reconciliation. It is not about barriers and boundaries, but about the embrace of God's love. And if this is so, to perpetrate division is to fly directly in the face of the gospel Paul seeks to proclaim. The entire congregation belongs to *Christ*, who incarnates the God who is creator of the whole world. The *historical Jesus* proclaimed a message to which the idea of community was central, and Paul continues to proclaim this message. It would falsify his gospel, constitute a practical denial of its meaning and effectiveness, if the church at Corinth persisted in nourishing the spirit of division.

The penchant for violent confrontation and rigid boundary maintenance that sapped first-century Israel's moral integrity and threatened its survival are painfully familiar to us, I suspect. We are heirs of the transformation effected by Jesus, and the God whose grace we meet in history has not, we may pray, abandoned our world. But the call to inclusive community he issued still finds few hearers, even in places in which Christian faith is proudly owned as an identity marker. When a best-selling Christian author proudly announces that he "bleed[s] red, white, and blue" at a time when doing so unavoidably implies endorsement of American jingoism, we may wonder whether Jesus' Capernaum message is any less relevant today than in the first century.

It is a good thing indeed to cherish our communities and our roots, to be loyal to the places from which we've come. But this kind of loyalty can too easily degenerate into fearful rejection of those who are different and hostile attacks on those who seem to threaten our way of life. Oppression and violence are not trivial, and they are worth resisting. But as those who have heard an inclusive gospel, we know that other things are worthwhile, too. The beauty of God of which the psalmist writes can be seen with special clarity in the creation of communities from which rejection and exclusion are absent. As we cherish those things that make our own national and local communities special, may we nonetheless recognize the importance of making their boundaries porous? May we hear anew the call to repent: to make our communities, including our global community, ones in which all are welcome.

31
Hospitality to the Stranger

As reading Hebrews 13 emphasizes, hospitality to the stranger should be a fundamental theme in the Christian life. There are at least two ways in which we can entertain strangers. We can invite new people into our social worlds. And we can come to a new appreciation of the essential strangeness of the people we regularly embrace with our hospitality. In brief, we can see friends as strangers and strangers as friends.

The language in Hebrews 13 about the purity of the marital bed veils a concern with continuing contemporary relevance. It is a reminder that those with whom we share our lives are strangers—that is, that they are not mere extensions of ourselves. They have needs and rights and claims and desires and feelings of their own, and we cannot treat them as if there were no difference between their purposes and ours. The call to trustworthiness voiced in Hebrews 13 is a call to take their *strangeness* seriously.

People can be so close to us that we find it difficult to see them clearly. It is easy to take friends and lovers and partners for granted. The familiarity that results from their continued presence and the sense of security fostered by their implicit or explicit commitments to us can incline us to see them as parts of the furniture, backdrops to our various projects and undertakings, constituents of our support systems. To recall the real nature of our responsibilities to them, we must come at least sometimes to see them as aliens, as people who can surprise us. We must sense that behind the unremarkable faces at which we've looked over and over in the past are universes of feeling and experience and memory and hope and fear that we will never fully fathom. As we recall the strangeness of the seemingly close and familiar, we will recall that they may be affected by choices we would like to think of as casual—like the sexual betrayal contemplated in Hebrews 13—far more intensely than we would prefer to believe.

"It won't bother her. She'll get over it. What does it matter, really?" I suspect we've all said these sorts of things to ourselves more often than we'd care to admit, even if not in cases as dramatic as those alluded to at the beginning of Hebrews 13. To come to see the people we think we know as strangers is to take a crucial step toward acknowledging the inadequacy of these comforting bromides. Our friends are also strangers; and, whatever may be true of the phantoms of our imaginations, when *they* are pricked, they bleed.

We are also called to make friends, in some sense, of strangers.

Our lives are much simpler when we're dealing with people like us, people we know and understand. They don't challenge our self-perceptions. They don't force us to ask whether we need to change the ways we see ourselves and the ways we see our world. They allow us to continue living in cozy cocoons. Relationships, organizations, and societies are founded on ongoing acts of exclusion. Sometimes, we can see why drawing boundaries is necessary, even if not ideal. Limiting the number of students in a class enables the instructor to give each one personal attention. Maintaining a relatively small number of friends fosters the development of close, deep relationships with each. Commitments to emotional and sexual exclusivity help to enhance the intimacy, intensity, and durability of romantic relationships.

It's obvious, I think, that drawing boundaries isn't always so benign, however. Too often, we turn strangers into scapegoats or treat social outsiders as non-persons whom we can expect to bear costs we would never impose on ourselves. Think of the ways in which our institutions deny homeless people opportunities to care for themselves and improve their circumstances and even, too often, the right to sleep undisturbed in public spaces. Think of the ways in which those institutions continue to tell members of ethnic, cultural, and sexual minorities that they don't belong.

This kind of marginalization was very much a part of Jesus' social world. The accepted rules of social interaction and the policies actively pursued by those in power kept the pure and the impure, the wealthy and the poor, Israel and the nations, the insiders and the outsiders apart. But Jesus said *no* to exclusion, and *yes* to hospitality. In Luke's Gospel, he calls his hearers to a hospitality that says no to exclusion and rejection. *Break out of the cycle of reciprocal giving and receiving*, he says. *Forget about expecting a* quid pro quo. *Instead of propping up a social system that depends on a fine balance between what you give and what you get, offer a place at the table to those who can't pay you back.*

Some Christian groups have created comprehensive alternative social worlds, complete with educational institutions, hospitals, and industries, in which they can feel at home. There can be something genuinely warm and reassuring about such worlds. But the same structures that can make some people feel at home can help to create a new class of outsiders. People who, for one reason or another, don't measure up or fit in can end up ostracized, excluded, by tight-knit communities of faith—rejected and marginalized in ways earlier Christians would have found painfully familiar.

The Gospel tells us that divine love spreads for us a banquet, that God seeks to feed us "with [the] finest of wheat," "with honey from the rock." It tells us that God offers us friendship, an opportunity to celebrate, a place we can call home. It affirms, in the words of Deuteronomy quoted in Hebrews, that God will never leave us, never forsake us. What if the Christian church became known as a community that celebrated this kind of good news? What if it became known, not as a community perpetually hiding behind institutional walls, afraid of pollution from the outside world, but as a community that distinguished itself from other churches and from the surrounding culture by its practices of hospitality? What if it became known as a community that challenged and encouraged us to see the people to whom we're close as strangers, full of sometimes unsettling, sometimes delightful surprises? What if it became known as a community that challenged and encouraged us to see the people with whom we think have nothing in common as guests and potential friends? Suppose the church became known as the one place in a racially divided community where people from different backgrounds could sit peaceably at table? Suppose the church was in the forefront of heeding Luke 14 by challenging social institutions to invite homeless people and other wandering strangers to take their places at the table? Suppose that in Christian communities, women and sexual minorities felt more rather than less empowered and respected than they are in the wider society? Just suppose . . . .

The shape of appropriate hospitality to the friends who are also strangers and the strangers embraced as guests will obviously vary from situation to situation in ways none of us can anticipate. We can, however, be certain that hospitality is the essence of the Gospel. As we come to see the precious and surprising uniqueness of those to whom we are close and those whom we might wish to keep at a distance, as we welcome both into a liberating and celebratory hospitality, we come more fully to understand and embody the love of the God who invites us to the feast.

32
A New Humanity

The great work of Jesus, Ephesians proclaims, is the creation of a new humanity. Two millennia after Ephesians was written, that work is still under way, and very much incomplete. But we have every reason to be excited by what has already occurred.

We value familiarity. We trust familiar people and familiar places. And we know how to navigate familiar cultural environments. By contrast, we may find ourselves unsettled by strange ways of speaking and acting, of marrying and eating and working and worshipping. We may not be sure what to make of unfamiliar smells and accents and skin colors. And so we often find it easy to exclude and reject those who are different. Life may feel easier in their absence.

And there's a further wrinkle. Sometimes, we may subordinate members of other groups, robbing or enslaving them. And, when we do, our consciences may nag at us. Are they any different at a deep level from us? They don't seem to be. And so we may find ways to accentuate and underscore their differences in order to claim that these differences *justify* our domination of them. In this case, it won't just be true that we shun those who are already different because of their unfamiliarity; it will also be true that we emphasize others' differences in order to excuse ourselves for mistreating them.

Relatedly, even if we don't already think of others as undesirably different, even if we aren't already dominating them, we may imagine that we are special, entitled, in a way that authorizes us to turn others into subordinates. When a group thinks of itself as chosen by God, it can use this sense of specialness as an excuse for conquest and exploitation. As my friend and colleague Wonil Kim has emphasized, this kind of mentality seems evident in early Israel's understanding of its own presence in Canaan. And one doesn't need a biblical scholar to note the prevalence of the same attitude in the contemporary Middle East. But this kind of troublesome mentality isn't the province of any one community or tradition. Years ago, my best friend gave me a book examining the ways in which different countries have understood themselves as chosen by God: this attitude has persisted across the globe. The United States and Russia, for instance, have both understood themselves as motivated by divine commissions.

The idea of a divine covenant with Israel, evoked in both 2 Samuel 7 and Psalm 89, need not be understood as dependent on or supportive of any commitment to ethnic superiority or arbitrary divine favoritism. The best way to think about this covenant, I think, is as a matter of God's taking advantage of history. The ongoing, interweaving pattern created by the combination of divine providential nudges, human freedom, and historical and physical accident creates ever-new possibilities for God's self-disclosure. As Israel's religious tradition developed, it became an increasingly effective vehicle for the transmission of a genuinely universal vision of a God of justice and inclusive love. Like all ideas, like all insights, this vision had to come from *somewhere*. It had to have roots. Both its initial discovery and its transmission required a home, a specific tradition. But the idea of ethical monotheism pushes beyond any particular geographic locus, prompting an understanding of the whole world as the locus of God's activity and focus of God's grace. The covenant here is not a special privilege for any ethnocultural group; rather, it reflects what particular historical circumstances make it possible for God to do as a way of blessing all of humanity.

In Mark 6, Jesus' disciples are sent out to preach. Initially, their mission is local. But the compassion Jesus feels for those who are "like sheep without a shepherd," the care he exhibits for those who are sick, differentiated simply by their illnesses, not by ethnicity or religion or class, points toward the universality of the mission Jesus' ministry ultimately models and inspires, as his followers spread throughout the ancient world.

Ephesians highlights the results of that preaching. What, for the epistle, has Jesus accomplished? "For he himself is our peace, who has made the two groups one and has destroyed the barrier, the dividing wall of hostility, by setting aside in his flesh the law with its commands and regulations." The point is not, of course, that *morality* goes out the window, but rather that Jews and Gentiles can form one community even as their cultural particularity remains intact. The focus need not be on the physical temple David proposes in 2 Samuel to build for God, who, as infinite and omnipresent, does not live in finite physical structures; rather, it can and should be on the new community being founded on an inclusive vision of grace, a community that can be described as a household, a building, a temple, a dwelling. This is the radical liberation we celebrate and experience anew in the Eucharist, in the communion service, as we come together in grace to (re)form a new community, revealing in powerful ways what grace means, helping to transform the world by modeling a distinctive and powerful way of being together despite our differences.

Of course, even this temple, this dwelling, cannot contain God, of course. Just as God cannot be localized to a physical temple, so God cannot be isolated to a particular community. John 1 stresses that the *Logos* is "the light that enlightens everyone." As the great second-century Christian advocate Justin Martyr wrote, Christ "is the Word of whom every race of men were partakers; and those who lived reasonably are Christians, even though they have been thought atheists . . . ." As with the covenant with Israel, so also with the covenant with the church: talk about covenant shouldn't make us feel superior; rather, it should simply call attention to the opportunities our distinctive historical position creates for God to use us to bless the entire world with whatever insights divine grace can use us to convey, with whatever healing divine grace can use us to offer.

33
The Still, Small Voice

In a short story, Woody Allen purports to quote someone as beginning a narrative by saying: "I was flying my private Cessna from New Mexico to Amarillo, Texas, to bomb some people whose religious persuasion I do not wholly agree with." One of the multiple sources of amusement here is the unblinking, unthinking cold-bloodedness in evidence.

We chuckle, and rightly so. But as we recall the Bible's evocative depiction of God as addressing Elijah in a gentle whisper—in a "still, small voice"—it's worth remembering that he's in hiding because he's just killed a great many people because he didn't share their religious views.

The point is not that his opponent, Jezebel, is a remotely attractive character. She is herself utterly cold-blooded, willing to bring about the judicial murder of a man to ensure that his property can be rendered available as a vegetable garden for her husband. Violence is part of the scene in the Israel of Elijah's time. But Uncle Arthur's Bible stories don't hold up Jezebel as a model for anyone; they do, however, laud the character of Elijah. And, while we have good reason to affirm courage and the commitment to Israel's well being he is depicted as exhibiting, we should still be troubled, it seems to me, by his remembered use of lethal force—not to defend the defenseless, but to eradicate those he judged to be false prophets.

Elijah is hardly alone. We don't like to be challenged. When people disagree with us about things that matter, the very fact that we do so can be unsettling, and we can find ourselves instinctively striking out.

It is a mistake, I believe, to suppose that all religious communities are saying the same thing, or that the claims made by all traditions are equally correct. To say this is to miss the complexity of different traditions' actual recommendations for individual and communal life, and their actual impact on culture and society. Religious disagreements may be profound and powerful, and they may implicate the most fundamental questions about authority and justice. Think, for instance, about the debate over slavery in mid-nineteenth-century America.

So, in asking about our concerns regarding Elijah's killing his opponents, I am not suggesting that we should ignore religious disagreements. I do, however, want to suggest several things as we think about these disagreements.

First, God is the creator of everything that is. The divine word, the *Logos*, spoken of in John 1 as incarnate in Jesus, is the source of the order and meaning of the entire universe—that is what the idea of the *Logos* is in the neo-Platonic philosophy that forms the backdrop to John 1. And the prologue to the First Gospel describes that Word as "the light that enlightens everyone." And, finally, God's Spirit moves over the face of the waters, of the chaos of the world. God's Spirit is active in and through all creaturely events, though creatures retain their freedom and integrity. The bottom line: God is present and efficaciously active everywhere, and that means that there is no place, no district of thought, action, experience from which God is absent. Different traditions may get it more right than others about various issues, but God is there wherever we are.

Second, our Psalm notes that cry from the heart for God on the part of the psalmist. This is an aspect of all human lives, Augustine argued: a longing for the infinite, for a secure ground for our existence. We may not know it, the Augustinian tradition has said, but this longing, a pervasive feature of human experience, is a longing for God. It's not just something experienced by people who agree with us.

Third, the gospel, the good news of God's love conveyed in the words and deeds of Jesus, is the good news of a divine love that is not tied down to human structures and that includes people without distinction. As regards structures: this is the message—or, at any rate, a message—Paul seeks to convey in Galatians 3. The law here is not the moral law as a means of salvation; it has never been the case that God accepted people on the basis of their performance. No, Paul's focus here is perhaps best seen as on the law as an identity marker. The persistent question with which he wrestles is, Must one be a Jew in order to be a Christian. The law is that which delineates the boundary of the covenant community. Paul's answer to his own question seems to be clear: God has not rejected or abandoned the Jewish people (see Rom. 9-11), but being a Christian isn't the same thing as being a Jew, and it is important to distinguish between what is needed to be a faithful Jew and what is needed to be in right relation to God. The law, the covenant boundary-marker *isn't* what's decisive.

And note what Paul goes on to say: in light of the divine love revealed in Jesus, we can see that distinctions between people based on ethnicity, social class, or gender simply aren't decisive. We are all embraced by God's love. We can envision a community that incorporates all of us. The list he offers here is, I think, illustrative rather than exhaustive. The point is *not* that people may be one whether they're male or female—but only if the division between them reflects factors other than varying religious views, sexual orientations, or political ideologies. No: God's love is inclusive. Paul's focus is on oneness through baptism, but I think this makes the most sense if it's understood as a reflection of what is the case whether people are baptized or not: we are all God's creatures, all valuable, all valued by God. And that's as true of Jezebel and her prophets as it is of Elijah and his allies.

To repeat, that doesn't mean that, when religions practice child sacrifice or mutilate the bodies of women or encourage quietism or caste hierarchies or discrimination, their behavior is acceptable. They can and should be opposed and challenged. But, even when people make horrible, destructive mistakes, even when we need to oppose and restrain them, even when we need to defend others against injustice, if necessary by force, we need not view those with whom we disagree as The Enemy, irredeemably blind or evil. We have no warrant to murder our opponents—literally, as Elijah did, or symbolically, as we often do with our words and actions.

Instead, we can begin with the recognition that God's creating, redeeming, inspiring activity isn't absent from any life. It's easy to be terrified of people who are different from us. But when we actually engage with the Other, when we discover who she or he really, we will discover—as we see so dramatically in the Gospel story of the demoniac—that underneath a potentially terrifying façade is the authentic humanity of another child of God.

Vulnerability and Community

When we embrace those who are different, those with whom we disagree, instead of trying to eradicate, subjugate, dismiss, or ignore, God can use them to surprise us, to challenge us, to help us break through our prejudice and self-imprisonment. Perhaps it is in the surprising voice of the other that we can most clearly hear the still, small voice of God.

34
Surprising Forms of Grace

It is, indeed, as the psalmist affirms "good and pleasant" when genuine community happens. Like falling dew, it offers new life, welcome vitality in the midst of a parched desert. Community—in the setting of a marriage, a friendship, a congregation, a workplace, a school—feeds our souls.

The psalmist compares the experience of falling dew with the achievement of "unity." And sometimes when we hear this word, we think of sameness. We suppose that community happens when people act the same way, think the same way, feel the same way.

It's understandable that we might reason like that. After all, it is often the case that those who disagree judge and condemn and reject each other. The very existence of someone different from me can seem to constitute and unsettling challenge to me: Justify yourself! And it's hard to imagine experiencing community with someone who's judging and attacking me all the time.

It is not surprising that, in John 20, we find the disciples hiding for fear of the Jewish leaders. For Jesus's public ministry seems to have been experienced consistently as a challenge to his contemporaries, some of whom reacted aggressively.

His inclusive, grace-filled practice may well have served as a persistent challenge to styles of faith and culture that treated drawing boundaries between insiders and outsiders as absolutely crucial. Jesus didn't have to argue or confront, though of course he seems to have done just this on occasion—he simply had to extend grace, to show in practice what it looks like to welcome those who don't fit in.

His extension of grace to people who didn't look or act in the way religious leaders thought they should made clear that the sky wouldn't fall if outsiders were welcomed with open arms. And there are few things as unsettling as a practical demonstration that there are really alternatives to the dominant consensus. Abstract arguments can be refuted or ignored; but showing, really showing, that things don't have to be the way they are can break the bars that constrain people's imaginations, helping them to envision—and build—a better world.

But of course for the people with a vested interest in this world, in the established order, that can be profoundly threatening. And it is easy, all too easy, to respond to what threatens us by attempting to erase it. No doubt Jewish and Roman leaders worked to arrange Jesus's death for multiple reasons; but among those reasons, I suspect, was the desire to eliminate a threateningly dramatic depiction of the live possibility of another world.

Grace comes to us by breaking us out of our self-created prisons. God graces us by offering the gift of otherness. And of course that's not a one-time gift. Over and over we need to be surprised by the discovery that we're not at the center of the universe and that our assumptions and biases and deeply held convictions need to be nuanced and stretched and enriched and sometimes abandoned, and that we ourselves can matter even if our value doesn't trump that of everyone else. Jesus offered the grace of otherness to his contemporaries, and he was killed for his pains.

We find otherness unsettling even in less dramatic contexts. So it's not surprising that, when we think about the achievement of unity that is as refreshing as oil running down the beard of Aaron (if we can get past the fact that this is a simile that's unlikely to move us!), we think of eliminating difference. In John 20's depiction of Jesus's appearance to his disciples after his death, he repeatedly offers peace. We want peace, but we often want peace that's marked by freedom from the challenge of difference. We want "unity" understood as sameness. Sameness feels safe.

But as Annette Baier observes, safety and love don't fit together well. "It is not very 'safe,'" she says, "to love another. If safety is what one values most, the womb or the grace is the best place for one, and, between the two, one will want the best approximation one can get to those places where one is sheltered from or beyond hurt." One will opt, that is, to avoid real engagement with others. One will opt for death over life.

Vulnerability and Community

People are challenged. People are broken. The point is made bluntly in 1 John: "If we claim to be without sin, we deceive ourselves and the truth is not in us. . . . If we claim we have not sinned, we make him out to be a liar and his word is not in us." Good people, decent people, compassionate people, loyal people mess up. They fail to embrace the reality that they are parts of God's good creation—that they are infinitely valuable and precious, and that, at the same time, others are equally real and equally valuable and precious. The very being of others forces us to think hard and pray hard and work hard—and their blindness and clumsiness and wrongdoing challenge us to understand, to forgive. Even when they choose virtuously, they see the world in different ways than we do. They challenge and unsettle.

We can experience community with such people, and others can experience community with us (we are such people, after all!). But community can't happen if we expect to build it on a foundation of sameness. This is because we can't experience the gift of otherness if we take this stance. It's also because people are in fact different—and that's OK.

Differences in an interpersonal relationships, as Hugh and Gayle Prather observe, "add to, rather than subtract[ing] from, the richness of the relationship." Reaching this realization depends, however, on "comfort with ourselves." To put the point theologically, if we know ourselves accepted and love by God, if we see ourselves as infinitely valuable parts of God's good creation, then we need not feel threatened by difference. By contrast, if we're not sure about our own value, we may rely on the perceived need to be right to shore up our sense of who we are, and, if this is the case, we may push back violently at differences that challenge us.

Christian counselors Henry Cloud and John Townsend observe, in their best-selling book *Boundaries*, that couples, in particular, frequently

> feel distress over the differences between them. They will say, "I don't see how we ended up together; we are so diametrically opposed." These polar extremes can run the gamut, from theology to politics, from career to sex, from family to finances, intimacy to entertainment.
>
> . . . Being different should not be a problem in marriage. In fact, it should be a benefit. When your mate has an alternative viewpoint to yours . . . , you have been enriched. Your world has been enlarged. You

are no longer bound to a world of your own making, which is a prison God never intended for us. You are forced to listen to, interact with, and consider the feelings and opinions of another human being in some matter in which you are dead sure you are right. If this is not a solution to human arrogance, what is!

The early Christians in Jerusalem sought, according to Acts 4, to craft a kind of community in which difference was minimized, with property given over to the community for administration. My distinguished former colleague George T. Simpson hypothesized that this abandonment of individual ownership was partly responsible for the economic crisis in the Jerusalem church to which the charitable collection in which Paul is reported at various points in the New Testament to have engaged was a response. Whether Professor Simpson was correct, it's clear that a model of community in which difference and separateness are drastically reduced, especially an extended community—a church is neither a family nor a group of friends on a camping trip, and neither is a neighborhood or a workplace of a city—can prove problematic in multiple ways.

Learning to deal with individuality, with difference, is difficult. It's easier, simpler, to opt for sameness, to reject or ignore those who differ with us, to avoid the challenge they pose. But the only kind of unity we can enjoy with real people while understanding them clearly and engaging with them fully is unity that comes when we accept and embrace each other despite our differences. We can have unity in diversity, unity without uniformity. And this kind of unity allows real community to happen, since we are, in fact, different, and without real openness to difference we will not fail to experience the grace of otherness but also condemn ourselves to isolation or the quest for those who are, conveniently, just like us, while missing out on the challenge, the delight, the sizzle of those who unsettle and surprise us.

This kind of unity really is, in the psalmist's language, a "blessing," "life forevermore." And, as Baier reminds us, while "[t]here is no safe love," nonetheless "the relations of interdependency and our responses to them . . . [are] big with the promise of strengths united, of new enthusiasms, of special joys, of easy ungloved intimacy, of generous giving and forgivings, of surprising forms of grace."

Part IV
Providence and Vulnerability

35
Rejoicing without the Messiah?

"Rejoice always," Paul instructs the Thessalonians. And it is difficult to imagine an injunction seemingly less reasonable. For why should we rejoice, when disease assaults our bodies and the bodies of those we love; when political elites and their cronies steal the property of poor people and deny them opportunities to better themselves economically; when wars claim the lives of many and the innocence of more; when hatred and suspicion stand in the way of love between persons and between peoples?

We know the answer we are supposed to give, of course. We remind ourselves to rejoice. "Joy to the world—the Lord is come." But what can this mean? In what way is the activity of Jesus cause for joy?

Judaism's principal complaint against Christianity has been precisely this: if the Messiah has arrived, why does history go on as it has for millennia? Why are innocents still crushed by the juggernaut of tyranny?

John the Baptist finds joy in the coming of the Messiah. "Among you stands one whom you do not know, the one who is coming after me; I am not worthy to untie the thong of his sandal." John finds a sense of meaning and purpose as he takes part in the mission of the One whose coming he heralds. But despite that mission, the world seems dangerously similar to the one John knew, a world in which we die, disappointed and apparently alone.

It is salutary to remember that the Jesus John proclaimed was no stranger to the bleakness of our existence. Perhaps the defining moment of Jesus' career was his cry from the cross: "My God, my God, why have you forsaken me?" It is in this Jesus that Paul tells his readers to rejoice. What a strange joy this then is.

For the author of Psalm 126, in one of the most beautiful passages in the Bible, deliverance made the people of Israel "like those who dream," their mouths filled with laughter and their tongues shouting joy. Joy comes through salvation—and not an anticipated future salvation, not a present but private change in consciousness and disposition, but a transformation of the public world, the world of kings and battles and harvests. In this world, Israel has come home. And so it is in this world that the people of Israel rejoice.

For Paul, too, the world is different because of Jesus. In what did Jesus' victory consist? It is, among other things, the tangible creation of a new community. The concrete life of the community of faith, its sharing, its commitment to inclusion and to justice—that this new common life has been brought into the world is cause for rejoicing. History *is* different, in a way.

Perhaps the same sense that redemption happens in people's lives, here and now, lies behind the words we read in Isaiah 61. Isaiah envisions God as offering Israel a renewed and eternal covenant. And it is this that leads to rejoicing. But before the covenant is mentioned, the concrete practice of the community comes into view. The "year of the Lord's favor" is marked by provision for "those who mourn in Zion." It is marked by the repair of devastated cities. It is marked by the announcement of liberation to the oppressed, comfort for the brokenhearted, and freedom for the enslaved. While the return of Israel from captivity may be the primary focus of this passage, the image of the jubilee, which promised solidarity and equality for Israel, is clearly in view as well. Joy happens because salvation has occurred or will occur in history.

But if this is so, then we must give serious thought to the nature of our rejoicing. For if we are called to rejoice; if joy follows on the transformation of our own and others' lives in this world; and if this transformation cannot happen—as it seems clear that it cannot—apart from us, then we have much to do.

We cannot turn the gospel into an occasion for works righteousness. Verbal sleight of hand cannot eliminate the fact that we are called to rejoice in what has already been done for us. At the same time, however, we cannot ignore the seeming absence of redemption from our experience.

We confess a God who attends with infinite patience to the particularity of each creaturely reality, and who is consequently enmeshed in our suffering, anguish, and futility. We see Jesus crushed by rejection, and we find in Jesus' suffering a pointer to God's vulnerable outreach to us. We see Jesus crucified, and we remember that the pain of the world is an ongoing crucifixion for God. Can there be joy in this? Can we rejoice?

Whatever joy there is must live deeper than the fractured surfaces of our broken lives. It must be real and meaningful in this world, the struggling world that is our home. It must be a joy we can experience with both eyes open. And thus the joy that we are cherished and desired, passionately loved, by a God who suffers, a God who is vulnerable, a God who can be rejected and hurt, whose purposes can be frustrated—this is the only kind of joy that could matter.

If we were called to rejoice in a deceptive messiah, a proponent of the naïve health and wealth gospel, we would have every reason to refuse, to condemn such a call as a destructive delusion. If we were called to rejoice in a divine love that delivered a chosen few from the terrors of earth while leaving terrestrial wounds unhealed, terrestrial chains unbroken, we would have every reason to dismiss the call as a narcotic designed to lull us into complacency.

But we are called to rejoice in a divine love that is immersed in the dirt, the destruction, the death of our own, real world. Whether the ancient theologians who termed Mary of Nazareth the *theotokos*, the God-bearer, chose the right term or not, they were right to emphasize that God cannot be insulated from the vulnerability associated with the process of birth, with childhood, with the terrors of being human.

And we are called to rejoice in a divine love that accepts this vulnerability and works with and in and through it to craft new communities of memory, resistance, and hope, new communities that can begin to make real the power of saving grace in our lives and the lives of our cities, nations, and world. Common life in Christ is not the only place where God's grace is apparent. And it is not a means of self-salvation, a strategy for earning divine favor. Rather, it is precisely the *actualization* of God's love in the world. It is what God's love looks like lived out. Proclaiming good news to the poor and comforting the broken-hearted does not *earn* salvation; it makes salvation real in the world.

If we are to rejoice, then, we must rejoice in a manner shaped by a picture of God suggested by the stories of the birth of Jesus in a noxious stall full of barnyard animals, the infant Jesus dependent on his mother, the baby Jesus who is depicted as fleeing the violence of

Herod, the Jesus with nowhere to lay his head but the straw of a borrowed manger. In these stories, we can discern windows on God's way with the world, God's identification with it in its vulnerability and suffering. And we can recall that God's loving union with the world gives birth not only Jesus but, through Jesus, to a community whose task—our task—is to make God's love real in the life of everyone, to show that because of Jesus, things *are* different. To know ourselves cherished, accepted, and inspired by such a love may give us the only cause to rejoice that will continue even amidst the darkness that still haunts us, even when we are called to rejoice.

36
The Opiate of the Masses

Karl Marx famously declared religion "the opiate of the masses." Was he right? Does hope anæsthetize us against the world's pain so we will leave oppressive structures undisturbed? If so, perhaps we should throw in our lot with Marx.

Whether it's healthy or not, hope can seem utterly unrealistic. Consider Isaiah's prophecy of future glory and restoration. The desert will become a garden. The sick will be healed, the exiles return. The timid may relinquish their fear. God is coming to vindicate and save.

To be sure, fools and the impure are excluded from the prophet's new Israel. The return to Zion will—we who know the story realize—lead to the exclusivistic abuses of Nehemiah and other, later, leaders. Divine vindication is spoken of as vengeance. But disregard these problematic elements. Most importantly, we must ask: *is deliverance coming?* Will the desert bloom? May we truly hope, or do promises like this merely lull us into passivity?

And what of the words of comfort we read in the Psalms? God, who is ever-faithful, delivers the oppressed, feeds the hungry, guards the migrant, defeats the unjust. But *are* the oppressed delivered, are the hungry fed, are the prisoners released?

James seems to recognize the dissonance between biblical injunctions to hope and the reality of oppression. But in response he offers only patience amid suffering. We should emulate the prophets: ignored, imprisoned, sawn in two, but faithful nonetheless. We must hope. But for what?

The theme of hope resounds from Genesis to the Apocalypse. We cannot abandon hope without eviscerating Christianity. But can we give voice to a hope that acknowledges the fact that we do suffer, that evil often seems victorious? And can we avoid becoming the proprietors of a kind of spiritual crack house, peddling narcotics to the oppressed and dejected?

The imprisoned John the Baptist doubtless finds hope difficult. He has spoken truth to power, and power has responded as it often does—by enforcing silence. Now, he waits. What can he expect from Jesus? Not, it appears, the forcible expulsion of Rome from Israel. Not the decisive restraint of the rapacious tax farmers who make the poor even poorer. Not the overthrow of the Herodians, the purification of the temple, or many of the other things he may expect Israel's restoration to involve.

At the Jordan he has pronounced a prophetic blessing on Jesus. But might he have been wrong? "Are you the one who is to come," he inquires, "or shall we look for another?"

We are all essentially in John's position. We see the fear in the faces of children terrorized by drone strikes. We listen to Palestinian and Israeli mothers mourning the deaths of soldier sons. We remember the atrocities of Latin American dictatorships and American policymakers' complicity in training their torturers. Closer to home, we watch our loved ones die and our marriages and friendships come apart. So we cannot but ask: "Are you the one who is to come, or shall we look for another?" As the Jew persistently queries the Christian, "If the Messiah has come, why is the world not redeemed?"

Jesus does not dismiss John's question or issue a peremptory demand for faith. Instead, he says: "Look and see." He does not announce that the Romans have been evicted from Palestine, that illness is no more, that social injustice has been done away with conclusively. But personal and social healing *is* taking place. Recall Jesus' comparison of God's reign to a developing mustard seed. Great things start small. Even if only in small ways at any given time, the human story is being transformed. In Jesus' words and deeds God's future is becoming present.

The most revelatory event of Jesus' career is perhaps his cry from the cross: "My God, my God, why have you forsaken me?" Jesus could testify to John that in his own actions God's will was being realized in history. But he could not count on a divine deliverance that simply abolished the contingencies of human life and defeated all evil. For us, the cross can symbolize God's vulnerability, the fact that God is not in the control business, that things often do not turn out the way God wants.

Vulnerability and Community

When we reflect on these matters during the Advent season, we are reminded of another symbol of vulnerability. We can see manger as a profound clue pointing to the character of God. We can see God not only in the dying man on the cross but in the bawling infant, totally dependent on others, seeking his mother's breast. There is nothing wrong with the warm fuzzies that often mark the Christmas season. But we must remember the absence of room at the inn for a poor family, the smell of animal droppings on stale straw, and the tread of soldiers on a grim and dreadful mission. Bethlehem, like Calvary, can serve as a pointer to divine vulnerability.

Suppose we take the lament from the cross and the cries of the impoverished infant as keys to understanding who God is. If we understand that God is not in the control business, that God's will is all too often *not* done, we can believe in a God of love despite the horrors of our lives. But can we still retain any reason for hope, a hope that is realistic about the reality of evil but that offers more than pie in the sky?

Think again about Jesus' words to John: right now, he says, things are changing. And change they did. From small beginnings, the Jesus movement transformed the world—not overnight, but over the course of centuries. We may continue to hope and work for real change. Sometimes, it may come with remarkable speed (consider the abolition of slavery or the embrace of same-sex marriage in America). Often, it will often be painstakingly slow. But real progress does happen. Relationships develop, wounds heal, corruption is rooted out, and new songs of freedom resound.

We can hope, too, for an attentive and loving divine presence that graces us even when, like John, we find ourselves destitute. Jesus' gentle message to John exemplifies the divine love that meets us even in the darkness of Herod's prison.

And we can hope for a future beyond death in which we may be cherished eternally by God and united with the rest of God's creatures in love.

Is this pie in the sky? It would be if it served as compensation for keeping our mouths shut in the face of evil. It would be if it lulled us into complacency and passivity. But it need do neither. The God we meet in Jesus does not offer us future hope as a pay-off for our acquiescence in the world's evils. By sharing them, God makes clear that they are not trivial, somehow irrelevant in the light of eternity. By offering a vision of renewed community as the focus of our hope, God inspires us to work for peace and justice now. By offering us hope beyond death, God gives us a reason for courage, a reason not to fear the death threatened by those who challenge justice and integrity.

The cross and the manger symbolize God's immersion in the vulnerability and suffering of history, God's confrontation with evil alongside us and through us. God offers no guarantees designed to cut the nerve of our opposition to oppression. God calls us to meet evil, not with the confidence that heavenly cavalry are prepared to deliver us if the battle gets too tough—if they are, why not simply send them on stage right now?—but in the conviction that, whatever happens, we are safe in God and that love and justice are the ultimate truth of things and deserve our passionate loyalty.

The answer to John's question and our own must thus be: "No, there is no other for whom to look." The vulnerable God of the cross and the manger is the only God there is. No substitute is waiting in the wings to step in to replace the God of vulnerable, persuasive love when the going gets especially tough. Are you the one who is to come? *Yes*. And the one who is to come is the one who has *already* come, in weakness and vulnerability—offering no panaceas, but a patient and loving presence with us and for us in the midst of chaos, suffering, injustice, and loss. The one who is to come and is here invites us to participate in the triumph of love, a triumph that is even now growing among us, small as a mustard seed.

37
God in History

"God reigns," says the psalmist. "Let the nations tremble." God "is exalted over all the nations." God "loves justice" and has "established equity." God has "done what is just and right." Psalm 99 articulates an attractive and confident vision of God's sovereignty over history. For the psalmist, God governs the affairs of nations in ways that foster justice. There is order in history and in international affairs.

This vision has had powerful consequences for the way in which people in our culture feel about the world. If God rules the nations, Christians and Jews and Muslims have maintained, then there must be order in history. History must be a context in which we can see who God is and what God intends. The world must be headed somewhere. Genuine novelty and advance will be apparent, because that God seeks the well being of the world.

We cannot be certain about the historical roots of the attitude toward history evident in Judaism, Christianity, and Islam. Its source may lie in the storied call of Abraham, challenged to abandon his family home and strike out into the unknown. Israel's recollection of deliverance from Egypt may also have played a crucial role. Jewish families and communities and congregations repeated the narrative persistently: not in the temple of the heart, not in a future beyond death, but in the present, a rag-tag fugitive army of slaves throws off the yoke of their oppressor in response to what they hear as God's summons. God acts in and through their escape from Egyptian dominance. The prophets underscored the belief that God's will was evident in history as they situated the vicissitudes of international politics in the context of divine providence. Because God was the ruler of the nations, what happened to Israel could be understood as divine blessing or divine judgment.

For Christians, the sense that history is the place where God's presence and activity can be detected is grounded in the story of Jesus. A community that confesses that God has done something new, something decisive, in a particular time and place, in the story of an itinerant Galilean rabbi, must regard history as vitally important. And the Christian conviction that there is meaning in history, that God rules the nations, has continued to shape the practice of Christians and others in the West.

Perhaps the view that God is ultimately in charge should have led to fatalism about history, but it seems in general that it has not. Instead, it has unleashed the energies of generations of people who have sought to change the world, confident that how things are is not how things are fated to be. But what are we to make of it? How can we understand it now, in an era that has witnessed the atrocities of Stalin, Mao, Pol Pot, and Hitler and the bombing of Hiroshima?

The events that have transpired since September 11, 2001, in particular, raise unavoidable questions about this understanding of God's role in history. Could the small son of a mother who died because she chose to make a brief visit to the World Trade Center on September 11 say with conviction that God rules, that God has done what is just and right? What about the daughter who lost a father when US forces in Afghanistan mistakenly attacked and killed troops loyal to the Afghan government in the village of Haraz Qadam?

Our options are limited.

First, we can take the psalmist's vision of divine sovereignty as the exclusive and all-sufficient statement of the biblical and Christian view. Maintaining that God is in control, that providence disposes the affairs of the nations, we can see the violence, the bloodshed, the loss of our era as God's will. This, we can say, gritting our teeth, is what divine justice looks like in our world. But, given the mercy of which the psalmist speaks, the love to which the Gospel testifies, it is hard to see how we could straightforwardly identify the destruction of human life and hopes and dreams, as the shape of God's justice in history.

Second, we can simply throw up our hands in dismay, concluding that God's will cannot be evident in the awfulness of our world at all. In this case, we can either abandon trust and hope in God entirely or opt for a spirituality of escape, seeking a God beyond our world who is essentially a stranger, an alien, rather than the Creator whose love and intention lie at the root of every actuality. No one can or should be blamed for choosing this second option. History often seems too awful to warrant continued hope. But I am not sure we are required to take this path.

This is so because, I think, there is a third option. Retaining our hope in God's goodness, we can attempt to discern and articulate an alternate understanding of God's work on behalf of justice in history, equity among the nations. One clue to such an understanding, I think, is found in the story of Jesus. Whatever else we make of the narrative of the Transfiguration, we can read it as a reminder that we see something important about the character of God when we look at Jesus. To identify Jesus as God's Son, to listen to him, is to find in him an evocative picture of God. And the picture of God we discern on Jesus' cross is not, I think, a picture of a God who is the untroubled ruler of history. If we speak, with 2 Peter, of witnessing God's majesty in Christ, we must do so with a sense of the paradoxical sense of what this majesty means. It may be appropriate to speak of Jesus as sovereign; but Jesus is enthroned on the Cross, and, in Nicholas Lash's pregnant phrase, "the paradigm of divine action in the world is the passion of the Lord's anointed."

Jesus' cross tells us that suffering is not God's will, that it is not how God does justice. For in the story of Jesus we see God confronting the evil that is responsible for so much suffering, not as an ally but as an adversary. And in the suffering of Jesus we see a pointer to God's own suffering, the suffering of One who teaches us not by deploying pain and evil as means of discipline but by enduring them along with us. Suffering is not God's judgment on the wicked; this is true whether the suffering in question is visited by terrorists on New Yorkers or by Americans on Afghans.

The sovereignty of a God identified in something like the way suggested by the story of the crucified Jesus is not the sovereignty of a God who sits in unruffled splendor above a world effortlessly governed in its minutest detail by divine power. It is the sovereignty of evocative, persuasive, empathic love. Persuasive love can slowly, patiently nudge and lure and shape the affairs of nations. It can impart order to human history. It can foster prosperity through trade and extended social cooperation. It can lead to the advances we see in a variety of areas of human life, advances whose significance for women, for the poor, and for others without power we should not underestimate. But, resisted at every turn by human fallibility, finitude, and sin, persuasive providence does not guarantee that God's will is done at every juncture. If God's sovereignty is *this* kind of sovereignty, then inequity and suffering will be evident even as divine providence continues to foster justice in our world.

There is something reassuring about the idea of a God who is always in control. But I do not think we can detect the image of such a God in a crucified man crying out, "My God, my God, why have you forsaken me?" To see God in the story of this man is to see a God we can confess as powerful only if we reconceive divine power as the power of persuasive love.

38
Dry Bones, New Life

In exile, Israel seems dead. Devastated by invasion, cut off from its homeland, it is as dry, dusty, lifeless as an array of skeletons. Everything seems hopeless. But, Ezekiel declares, just as the skeletons can be given new life, new breath, so Israel can come alive again, can return home.

New life, new breath, new hope. The psalmist prays expectantly, waiting for forgiveness and new possibilities. In Romans 8, Paul proclaims hope in the power of God: the power ultimately responsible for life beyond death, and the power at work to offer a new quality of life in the present. And Jesus as portrayed in John 11 surprises Mary, Martha, and Lazarus with new life.

Hope and renewal are persistent themes throughout the Bible and the Christian story. We don't talk about God's love and healing because things are going well. If there were no tumbles, no losses, no falls, no dispiriting defeats, no wrenching disconnections, no destructive eruptions of confusion and hatred and violence that leave us wondering if there is any reason to hope, the spiritual life would look and feel very different. Different traditions diagnose the underlying causes differently and prescribe different remedies, but all the varied wisdom traditions recognize the centrality of lack and, at the same time, the possibility of transcending loss and despair. The prospect of new life matters.

There are at least two temptations here—glibness and resignation. Glibness is the natural temptation of the stereotypical televangelist. No matter how dark the hour, no matter how great the less, the spiritually glib offer cheery consolation. Everything will be fine. God will wipe all tears away. Just have faith, and you'll have nothing to worry about.

Except, of course, that we do worry. We do know pain and grief and loss. And the announcement that we need simply to have faith unavoidably creates the suspicion that things wouldn't have gone wrong if I'd really trusted enough in God, trusted enough to . . . . To do what? To muster the right sort of emotional response? To banish internal doubts and worries? Only, apparently, if I make myself impervious to fear and concern will I have nothing to be afraid of or concerned about. By contrast, if things go wrong, it must be my fault. So I now have not only whatever loss I'm confronting to address but also a secondary problem, my own responsibility for what has happened. The glib claim to be offering comfort. But nothing they say seems very good, over the long term, at taking the pain away, and their overconfidence seems actually to compound it.

Resignation seems, by contrast, a measured and helpful response to loss. We accept that something awful has happened, and go on, finding diversions, trying to forget, hoping that we will stop being reminded, at some point, just how bad things have been. But resignation means giving up on hope. It means agreeing that things aren't going to get any better, and attempting to figure out how to manage given that they aren't. It means accepting the *status quo* as inevitable.

As Ezekiel's parabolic depiction of the valley of dry bones reminds us, it's unwise to give resignation the last word. That's true for at least two reasons.

First, to resign ourselves to pain and loss as inevitable means to close off the possibility of *doing something* ourselves about the challenges we face. Resignation means giving up, and therefore not striving to change things. And sometimes we *can* change things, even when it seems like we can't. But one thing seems certain: if we don't try, we don't succeed. Letting go of hope means letting go of the one thing that will often make change possible.

As the psalmist stresses, awareness of divine acceptance can matter here. Anyone who believes that God is love has no reason to pretend that that love is or could be available only when we realize it. But, when we do, we can see ourselves in a new way. Often, we have contributed in various ways to the defeats about which we are feeling hopeless, and we can berate ourselves, assail ourselves, without doubt and self-condemnation. Accepting that we are accepted can liberate us from the prison of our own self-recrimination, setting us free to keep trying to make change happen rather than accepting what has happened as some sort of inescapable punishment.

Second, when we resign, we let circumstances defeat us. But we may be doing so unnecessarily. Surprise is a genuine possibility. Deliberate choices by others, or the confluence of natural forces (and Christians will want to see God's providence at work in and through both), can transform situations in which we feel irredeemably stuck. Change really does happen. And our feelings of helplessness and defeat aren't always the best guide to what is and isn't possible. Hanging on to hope, even when don't feel hopeful, can make sense precisely because change may be waiting just around the corner.

Note that I said *may* be. That's the difference between hope and glibness. There are no guarantees. Anyone who has experienced defeat and loss knows that, even if divine love is at work in the world, as we hope and pray, this doesn't mean that it is at work *coercively*. If what we know of loss and brokenness is real—and only the glib would seek to brush it away—divine power is the power of persuasion, not coercion, and so works with the grain of the universe, confronting human fallibility and finitude and sin, working within the constraints of the natural order. We may pray that God's love be realized in the world precisely because it so often is not. We give ourselves and others no genuine comfort if we ignore this. We have every reason to puzzle, as Ezekiel does, over whether the dry bones will live.

Hope is not certainty. It is not sight. It is not knowledge. We can and should hope that, even when our circumstances are utterly bleak, the meaning of our lives may be secure in God's love and that there is hope for life, and transformation, in God even beyond death. But before we dwell on ultimates, on things that lie beyond our senses and our knowing, we have reason not to let go of the prospect of renewal, of liberation, in the present. Divine love, divine acceptance, can give us a new sense of who we are and of the value of our lives that can enable us to go one. We can and should hope, as I have said—because unexpected agencies of change can surprise us and because giving up hope means abandoning our own capacity to make change happen.

Israel, Ezekiel hopes, will come again to abandoned homes and once-familiar fields. The mournful loss of exile need not be the end of the story. May we, too, remember that dry bones can live unexpectedly, surprisingly—not embracing glib certainties but also not abandoning ourselves to hope-less resignation. May we wait and watch, work and hope, for breath and new life.

39
Treasures Old and New

Throughout much of the First Testament, there's a clear association between moral and spiritual performance and material prosperity. Consider Psalm 128: those "who fear the Lord," says the psalmist, "will eat the fruit of . . . [their] labor" and will experience "blessings and prosperity."[1] The message seems reasonably clear: righteousness brings a reward in the here and now. And the psalm focuses on the nation as well as the individual: it ends with the hope that Israel itself may know peace; and one reward for the righteous person will be the opportunity to "see the prosperity of Jerusalem"[2]— which it's easy to assume will result from a national righteousness paralleling the individual righteousness encouraged by the psalm.

Imagine the tension this kind of thinking must have created in first-century Israel. For many of Jesus' first-century Jewish contemporaries, the Exile had never really ended. Yes, Jews had returned to Israel after the relocation of their ancestors by occupying foreign powers. Yes, the temple had been rebuilt in Jerusalem. But the fact remained that Israel had been incorporated into Rome's empire. The authority of kings and high priests was overshadowed by the presence of a Roman governor and garrison. Israel's distinctiveness seemed to be eroding under the influence of Hellenistic culture. And the fact that God didn't seem to be doing anything about the nation's distress suggested that Israel was perhaps the object of divine judgment.

Jesus' contemporaries yearned for God to do something dramatic to vindicate their nation. As the prophets had seen God's hand at work in and through the processes of history, Jesus' contemporaries probably expected divine deliverance to take place by means of human action. For many of them, this meant revolution, holy war. For even more, it seems to have meant distrust of and separation from surrounding nations. Whatever their precise expectations, the vision of God's reign endorsed by Jesus' contemporaries tended to be nationalistic: it involved a commitment to the maintenance of a distinct Jewish identity, to separatism, to a vision of Israel as the special object of God's regard. It was linked with an oppositional view of other peoples and societies, one marked by hostility and defensiveness.

When Jesus talked about the "kingdom of heaven" (as in Matthew) or the "kingdom of God" (as in Mark and Luke), he wasn't talking about life after death, about God's reign in the distant future or in another dimension of reality. He was participating in his contemporaries' conversation about the restoration of Israel. He wasn't challenging their expectation that something remarkable was going to happen, that God was intent on acting transformatively in Israel's history; but he wanted to emphasize that what God was doing might not deliver what first-century Jews were anticipating. In particular, God wasn't in the business of underwriting nationalism and exclusivism. God was on the side of peace, not the side of holy war. God was at work in history—but unexpectedly. Jesus' parables help to explain his perspective.

The parable of the *mustard seed*, with its emphasis on great things coming from small beginnings, announces Jesus' conviction that, in Tom Wright's words, his "ministry . . . , which does not look like the . . . coming kingdom [his contemporaries expected], is in fact its strange beginning." It also trades on the fact that, as Dom Crossan notes, the mustard seed is a weed—dangerous and unpredictable. "[I]t tends to take over where it is not wanted, . . . to get out of control, and . . . it tends to attract birds within cultivated areas where they are not particularly desired." And the image of the birds coming to nest suggests, perhaps (here's Wright again), that "others, presumably gentiles, will to come to share in . . . [Israel's] blessing"—obviously a controversial thing to say at a time when holy war was in the air. The parable stresses, then, that God's activity is inclusive, unsettling.

The parable of the *leaven* suggests that what God is doing in Jesus' ministry is slow, patient, hidden, like yeast, but will ultimately yield dramatic change. Leaven is, of course, unclean, and women, too were, as Crossan observes, "associated in Judaism, as in other Mediterranean cultures, with the unclean, the religiously impure."[6] So the parable seems designed to unsettle expectations about purity and the social boundaries they were meant to sustain.

Israel had invested substantially in a particular understanding of itself as God's chosen nation. Preserving that understanding was vital, even if that meant rejecting outsiders and fostering talk about holy war that might—as Jesus anticipated—lead to Roman vengeance. The prophets had seen God's judgment in the actions of hostile foreign powers; Jesus seems to have discerned divine judgment in the anticipated violence of the Romans. Divine judgment would be executed by Rome: "Israel," Wright suggests, "is like fish in a drag-net, [with] good and bad [mixed] together, and soon the net will be on the shore and the bad fish thrown away . . . ."

Given the cost of maintaining its collective self-image and the boundaries and habits that went along with doing so, Israel would need to pay a high price if it chose to accept Jesus' new vision of God's reign—even if doing so was necessary to avoid Roman judgment. Jesus' called his nation to sell everything to obtain the pearl of great price, the treasure hidden in the field: Israel needed to abandon exclusivism, nationalism, a commitment to the idea of holy war. Wright summarizes: Israel's

> aspirations for national liberation from Rome, to be won through a great actual battle, were themselves the telltale symptoms of . . . [its] basic disease, and had to be rooted out. Jesus was offering a different way of liberation, a way which affirmed the humanness of the national enemy *as well as* the destiny of Israel, and hence also affirmed the destiny of Israel as the bringer of light to the world, not as the one who would crush the world with military zeal.[8]

Jesus offered, that is to say, a new conception of God and God's reign, continuous with Israel's traditions but nonetheless radical. Israel had a special place in God's plan for the world—precisely as a community that rejected nationalistic exclusivism.

The dramatic change Jesus anticipated has begun. His ministry, death, and life beyond death have unleashed a new dynamic in our world that has changed history irrevocably. We still look toward "the end of enmity and [to use Fritz Guy's evocative language] the ultimate triumph of love," and there is much that is bloody and awful in our world. But because of Jesus, things are different. Human history has taken a different turn. The old values of militarism and nationalism still hold sway in many societies and many hearts, but their mastery has been irreversibly undermined. As the parable of the mustard seed reminds us, God's work is not done overnight. Like Jacob working and waiting for Rachel, God continues to be active in human history—even if not in the decisive and overwhelming ways we might like.

As Paul affirms, nothing need separate us from the divine love we see in Jesus—but not because we will always know the blessings and prosperity the psalmist anticipated. Rather, the story of Jesus prompts the hope that the patient divine love we can see etched on the cross will accompany us into our darkest valleys. God remains present and active in all circumstances, even if sin and ignorance and unresponsiveness and accident get in the way. The image of the mustard see reminds us that while God is doing wonderful things, they don't happen overnight. God acts by persuasion, not coercion. Imperceptibly, surprisingly, like the mustard seed, peace and justice are happening: God's reign is growing. We face the challenge, as the parable of the householder reminds us, of drawing on our traditions, while discerning what God is doing in the present—of bringing forth treasures both old and new—as we seek to seek to help make God's reign a present reality.

40
Have No Fear!

"Take heart; it is I. Have no fear." Those words, spoken by the Jesus of the First Gospel as he crosses the storm-tossed sea, sum up the good news. I am uncertain how we should understand the historical details behind this narrative. But I am confident that the key elements of the story contain rich insights.

Jesus' disciples are frightened and tired as they make their way across the sea. The strange, ghost-like figure they see coming toward them hardly inspires confidence. Who or what is this?

But then, they realize that their eyes have been fixed on Jesus. Though rain, lightning, and distance may render him alien and frightening, they realize that it is their friend who is coming toward them across the water. "Have no fear," he tells them.

We fear too many things to count. We fear rejection. We fear violence. We fear being overwhelmed by the demands of others. We fear loneliness. We fear meaninglessness. And, in response to our fear, we scramble to secure ourselves in one way or another. We respond to our fear of loneliness by trying to control the people in our lives—trying to *force* them to be available to us. We respond to our fear of violence by preparing to be violent ourselves, and by shutting ourselves away from those we think are likely to harm us.

When we act out of fear, when we act out of a sense of insecurity, we are all too likely to act destructively or hurtfully, to frustrate the achievement of our own goals, to harm others or fail to see them clearly.

And so Jesus says to the disciples, "Have no fear." Just as they find it difficult to see him clearly, we obviously find it hard to see God clearly. The universe seems to be anything but a friendly place. We look through the storms of our lives, and we see, not a friend, but an alien, a foe, behind them. And so we act fearfully. And Jesus says, "Have no fear."

It's easy to turn this into pious claptrap. Every day, bad things happen to us, and to people we care about, and to strangers we don't know. "Have no fear" cannot mean, "Nothing bad will happen to you." Truly to reach a point at which we're fearless can't mean believing naively that our lives will be hassle-free. God's action in the world is persuasive, not coercive; thus, divine providence does not overmaster the brutality and destructiveness of life and ensure everyone a smooth ride. The Psalmist views Joseph's sojourn in Egypt as a gift of divine providence—after a judgment imposed by means of a famine. But we may wonder whether this sort of picture of God's meticulous providence is true to our experience of a world in God's will so often is not done. No, "Have no fear" is a meaningful injunction only if we understand it in another sense. We can be fearless if the fear we abandon is the fear that universe is at root an unfriendly place, that it lacks order and meaning, that we are adrift on a cosmic sea, without hope. "Have no fear" makes sense if it is a call to know ourselves loved and embraced by God, grounded and rooted in God, so that our lives are valuable and meaningful even if our circumstances are chaotic and painful. This isn't easy: we fall easily into fearful patterns; we feel anything but grounded. But at least this way of thinking about the fearlessness God offers us makes sense—it's not an absurd call to be Pollyannas.

The gospel, then, is a call to live out of this sense of groundedness, a call to see ourselves as truly at home in God—a call whose meaning the story of Jacob and Joseph helps to illuminate.

Parents have favorites. Sometimes a child will be preferred for being agreeable, or accomplished, or talented, or attractive. But sometimes, as in Joseph's case, perhaps all that matters is arriving at the right time.

Our connections and attachments are like that often enough. We bond with others not because our ties fit some cosmic blueprint, but because a history of interactions has taken particular twists and turns.

And reacting as Joseph seems to have reacted seems natural enough. Joseph relished his father's attention and affirmation. And the thought of his brothers prostrating themselves before them seemed so reasonable and appropriate that he seems not to have realized how offensive it might be to describe to them a dream in which it took place.

Jacob's older sons seem to have believed that they had to earn their father's approval, and they resented the easy grace with Joseph accepted and enjoyed it. Joseph rested secure in the knowledge that his father's love embraced him *no matter what*. Joseph knows himself at home in his father's love. His brothers—who have known Jacob as a difficult, demanding younger man "on the make"—have a different picture of their father. And the point is not to blame them. It isn't as if they're wrong. Jacob isn't God, after all: he's a human father, with all the flaws and foibles human fathers (and mothers) have in spades. But in Joseph's case, he's able to model a kind of acceptance that all of his sons *should* have enjoyed.

Before he is transformed in the crucible of Egyptian slavery, Joseph is not an admirable character. While we may envy his self-confidence, his insensitivity and unselfconscious egoism hardly make him a role model. But perhaps, ironically, Joseph's experience is not unrelated to the depiction of grace Paul offers in Romans 10. He contrasts right relation (this is what "righteousness" means in this context) with God "based on the law" with right relation "based on faith." It is not clear that Paul has in mind here quite the distinctions between works and grace that became especially prominent at the time of the Reformation. But we cannot help but think of those distinctions today when we read this passage. And those distinctions seem not altogether different from the divergent attitudes of Joseph and his brothers regarding their relationship with their father.

We may understand the achievement of right relationship through law as a matter of doing the right thing for the right reason. And it must be emphasized that doing the right thing for the right reason is very much to be preferred to the alternative. Jacob's older sons, we note, work hard for their father. Perhaps they do not always act out of optimal motives, but, in general, they do the right thing. But doing the right thing isn't what moves Jacob. Instead, what matters is a particular bond that links him with Joseph.

The gospel is the message that all of us are at home in God. And in this sense it is broad and general in nature, concerned with a generic feature of God's relationship with creation. But we pay no compliment to God if we act as if God is too busy or too exalted to attend to us in our particularity. The inability to do this is precisely a limitation, one unworthy of an infinite creator. God's love is not *partial*—it embraces everyone—but it is *particular*—engaging as it does with each of us as irreplaceable individuals. So Jacob's particular bond with Joseph, flawed as it is, provides us with an imperfect model of God's particular bond with each of us—a particular bond rooted not in what we *do*, something that can change and vary, something on which can hardly rely, but instead in who we *are*.

The phrase "Have no fear" encapsulates the message of the gospel. It tells us that the universe is a friendly place. It highlights, therefore, the possibility of a relationship with God in which each of us is loved and embraced in her or his particularity, in which each of us can come to feel truly at home.

41
Yearning and Connection

It is Paul the friend who is in view in 1 Thessalonians: the Paul we meet at the margins of so many of his letters, the Paul who, for all his fiery oratory, is someone who yearns for warmth and human connection, and who values rich interpersonal relationships deeply and dearly.

But the sense that God is in the testing business is also there in 1 Thessalonians, unfortunately, as it is in the book of Job. "God tests our hearts," Paul says, with the clear implication that he and his companions have passed the test. At Thessalonica, Paul and his friends can look back on painful suffering at Philippi. And perhaps Paul thinks of this as part of the test he has undergone. If Paul has not been through what the book of Job depicts its central figure as undergoing, he certainly knows, nonetheless, what it is to suffer. And his confidence in God doubtless has been tried as a result. But suffering has not broken him; it certainly has not embittered him. There is a rich, human warmth in his words. Paul and his companions seek to have been "gentle," "like a mother caring for her little children." "We loved you so much," Paul says, and "were delighted to share with you . . . our lives . . . , because you had become so dear to us."

What happens to Job is gut wrenching, the kind of thing that could reasonably be expected to destroy a person. But there is this similarity, that, like that of Bartimæus, the faith of Job makes him well, too, in a sense. And again, we can ask, is it that simple?

The accuser, the divine prosecutor, is invited to assess Job, to find out what he is made of, to test his heart. And Job stands firm, even though the testing process has left him devastated and almost broken. Despite everything, he remains convinced that God is God—too powerful, too great, too wondrous to comprehend. Before such a God, all Job can do is to bow. God is too overwhelming for Job to do anything but "repent in dust and ashes."

Just what are we to make of the sort of testing Job undergoes? Whatever later interpreters have suggested, there is little *in the book of Job itself* to suggest that the testing it narrates is undertaken for the benefit of anyone other than God. And God, we confess, knows the heart: there is no need for God to review the results of tests to determine what anyone is really like. Obviously, this God knows everything that an be known, requires no tests to discern who we are and what we are made of. But we can learn from the book of Job nonetheless, whether its vision incorporates everything the New Testament and later Christian reflection have wanted to say about God.

In the wake of this test, God, who knows the heart and honors Job, blesses Job, giving him "twice as much as he had before," prompting the renewed respect of his siblings, enlarging his flocks, and gracing him with new children, conveniently replacing those killed in the course of the test. And Job lives long.

The psalmist reports the same kind of deliverance. He vanquishes "all" his fears with God's help. The Eternal saves "the poor man" from "all his troubles." Not one of the good person's bones will be broken. God will "redeem the life" of the good person, ensuring that no one who takes refuge in God "will be condemned." And those who oppress him will receive their putatively just desserts: "[a]ffliction will slay the wicked, and those who hate the righteous will be condemned." Read together with Job, this passage might make us wonder what the force of expressions like "no one" and "never" might be. Certainly, it invites us to think about the confidence with which we might sometimes proclaim that divine deliverance will happen.

Bartimæus calls repeatedly, plaintively, to Jesus. Confidently, he reaches out, and Jesus tells him that his faith has healed him—with the result that he can see, and follows Jesus joyously. Simply told, direct, the story invites us to celebrate with Bartimæus, who dances after Jesus. But it also invites us to ask about the link between faith and deliverance. Is it really that simple?

For the psalmist, securing God's favor is as simple as being good. For Bartimæus, it is as simple as calling out.

There are few things better attested about the ministry of Jesus than that he was a healer, so I think we can affirm with some confidence that Bartimæus did, indeed, experience a healing touch that opened his eyes. But what about the suffering of Job, of the good person in the psalms? What about our suffering? It does not often seem to be remedied so quickly.

Imagine yourself undergoing what the book of Job portrays Job as suffering. Think about how you would view, feel about, your children, your partner. Perhaps your responses would be at least as intense as Paul's. We can certainly, in any case, agree that the presence of a new son or daughter in your life after the loss of another might be distracting, might well be wonderful in its own right, but certainly would not be *compensatory*. In the technical language of economics and law, your children, like Paul's friends, are not *fungible*. It's not the case that one will do just as well as another. While having more children ensures that you will be a fruitful patriarch, it does nothing to return to you particular children whom you have loved and lost. Certainly, for anyone with relational bonds as deep and important as Paul's, a replacement for a lost friend, even a doppelgänger, won't do.

Sometimes, when the plague isn't stopped, the drunken driver diverted, we look forward to a compensatory future: perhaps deliverance means compensation. But it seems to me that our instinctive reaction to what happens to Job might lead us to question the notion of divine deliverance as compensation. We would be right to do so. Just, I think, as we would be right not to seek meaning in suffering by viewing ourselves as the foci of some divine test. The God we meet in Jesus does not have lab rats.

It's anticlimactic, but the best we can do at such times, I think, is to see in the ministry of Jesus a God who is constantly seeking to heal, to liberate, while at the same time noting that the suffering to which the book of Job, Paul, and the psalmist all witness is evidence that divine power is the power of persuasion, not coercion, and that, too often, God's intentions are is not perfectly realized on earth. Not even close.

And we can see in the compassion of Jesus, mirrored, in a way, in Paul's yearning for connection, a pointer to the fact that God is, as Alfred North Whitehead said, "the fellow sufferer who understands." This God is neither a god who sets examinations nor a god who offers rewards for good behavior nor a god who treats children as replaceable. Rather, this is the God who is with us—at work for good in all things, but with us even when things aren't good after all.

This is a God who shares both our joy and our distress; who, as in Paul's phrase, embraces us gently, like a mother; who is, like Paul, delighted to share life with us because divine love finds us so dear.

42
"My God, My God, Why Have You Forsaken Me?"

"My God, my God, why have you forsaken me?" Christians have persistently affirmed the importance of seeing the character of God through the lens provided by the image of a young man dying, alone, on a cross—uttering these words. There are at least two potentially surprising aspects of the understanding of God and ourselves which this image suggests. Let's look at them: *suffering* and *power*.

In describing Jesus as "our high priest," the Letter to the Hebrews maintains that "we do not have a high priest who is unable to sympathize with our weaknesses, but we have one who has been tempted in every way, just as we are, without sin." Just a few verses later, we read: "Although he was a son, he learned obedience from what he suffered and, once made perfect, he became the source of eternal salvation for all who obey him . . . ." Hebrews stresses Jesus' unequivocal *identification* with suffering humanity.

Recall that, even as Hebrews describes Jesus as *made* perfect through suffering, it also describes him as "the radiance of God's glory and the exact representation of his being . . . ." For Hebrews, Jesus shows us what God is like. But this suggests, in turn, that being susceptible to suffering doesn't disqualify Jesus from providing us with a window on who God is. Indeed, if we treat the image of Jesus reciting the words of Psalm 22 as a clue to the identity of God, we can go beyond this: we can see susceptibility to suffering as a defining characteristic of God's nature. If in Jesus we can see something important about what God is like, then perhaps Jesus' vulnerability to suffering tells us something about *God's* vulnerability to suffering.

Some stereotypical views of God suggest that the capacity to suffer is unworthy of God. For proponents of these views, God is always active and never passive, always subject and never object. God acts; God is not acted upon. But to suffer is precisely to be an object. It is to be "on the receiving end" of others' actions. Those who have rejected the possibility of divine suffering while identifying Jesus as God incarnate have been forced to perform all sorts of logical gymnastics to explain how *Jesus* suffers even though, on their view, *God* cannot. They have seemed to affirm that God is, in fact, "unable to sympathize," even if, as in Hebrews, Jesus *is*.

There are multiple reasons for believing that God suffers. But I think it is clear that, if we understand Jesus as disclosing God, the suffering of Jesus can reasonably be seen as pointing to God's own suffering. And if we see God as suffering with us, as "the fellow sufferer who understands," we can perhaps find renewed hope and meaning in the face of our losses.

There are unavoidable risks associated with bringing into being creatures capable of great evil as well as great good and of natural processes and structures that can would and destroy as well as support. The suffering God is a God who is prepared to experience in person the consequences of taking those risks. The fact that God does so is not enough, of course, to *make* these risks worth taking. But it says something important about God's credibility—that God does not expose creatures to risks God does not wish to take Godself.

It also tells us something about our own lives. Vulnerability, the capacity to suffer, is absent from some common images of the ideal person, especially the ideal man. We are challenged to be tough, to shun feeling, to resist being affected. The conviction that God suffers, however, can only make us wonder about the appropriateness of this way of thinking. If God is vulnerable, if God loves—and therefore suffers—can we not do the same?

Understood as an image of or window onto God, the crucifixion of Jesus—of a man feeling dejected and abandoned enough to cry, "My God, my God, why have you forsaken me?"—tells us something about power as well as something about suffering. The image of the God who is capable of suffering is the image of a God who is not in control. The God who suffers with us is not a God who wipes away evil and destruction with a snap of the divine fingers. The power God exercises in the world is not the power of coercion; it is the power of persuasion. It is not the power of dominance; it is the power of love.

When we speak of God as perfect in power, we often imply that this means that God is in the domination business, at least in principle. And then, of course, we wonder why One with the kind of power we have imagined God as exercising doesn't sort out all of the world's problems, doesn't eradicate evil and suffering. The human beings we think of as powerful are typically those who can accomplish whatever they like. But God's power, this cry—"My God, my God, why have you forsaken me?"—suggests, isn't that kind of power. Again, the very experience of suffering and evil should teach us that, if God is good, divine power must not be coercive, but persuasive. But this powerful image points us starkly toward a different conception of power. This conception is, in fact, more compatible with our own experience of a world in which God's will is so often not done, a world in which we, like the crucified Jesus, so often feel forsaken by God. Like Job's, our complaints are sometimes bitter. But we can begin to respond to these complaints if we can endorse a conception of divine power framed in light of our recognition that the world's evils are not God's will, that God, like us, is their victim, not their perpetrator.

Jesus' suffering tells us not only about God's power but also about human power. The image of divine power as *dominance* disposes us, often enough, to think of the greatest human power, the most enviable human power, as the power to dominate. On this view, humans are most like God when they rule. But the image of Jesus crucified calls that assumption into question. It may prompt us to doubt, at any rate, whether hierarchical structures, organized in accordance with a command-and-control model, really count as anything like clear and decisive embodiments of God's goodness.

God's project, what God is up to in the world, turns conventional assumptions about power and status on their heads, as we are reminded by the disciples' puzzlement in Mark 10. If it is harder for a rich person to be part of God's project in the world—that, I take it, is what Jesus means when he talks about entering the reign of God here—than for a camel to pass through a needle's eye, "Who then can be saved?" they ask. If the rich, the most favored in society, find it profoundly difficult to be part of God's project, what about the rest of us? Traditional markers of power and status don't guarantee anything from God's perspective.

Of course, it is not just that Jesus *suffered and died* but that Jesus suffered and died *on a cross* that tells us something about power. He died the death Rome reserved for slave, aliens, rebels. Thus, the death of the innocent Jesus places a clear question mark against the condemnatory judgments issued by state authorities, against every choice by the state to deal out death and judgment.

The image of the suffering Christ points us toward the reality of a suffering God and challenges our own images of invulnerability. It undermines our own assumptions about power: that divine power is coercive power, that domination is an appropriate exercise of human power, that the power of the state is unproblematic. It prompts us to think in a new and more critical way about life in the world and about how the nature of the providential care of a loving but vulnerable God.

43
The Foolishness of the Cross

What made the cross foolish, as Paul suggests it was, or seemed to be? Perhaps there is a clue in his observation that the Greeks seek wisdom while the Jews look for signs.

The Gospel is foolishness to the Greeks because it says that *ultimate truth* is revealed in the agonizing death of a man on a cross. Not only was crucifixion a slave's death—and how could God be disclosed in an event involving a social nobody?—it was very much an experience of pain and vulnerability, of subjection to the accidents of history. Arguably, at least, for a certain kind of Greek thought, wisdom was a means of *escape* from vulnerability and accident. It gave one a place to stand outside the flux of history. If wisdom were found in a crucified man, didn't that mean an end to the search for a security beyond the world of chance and change? And mightn't it imply that we ourselves might be called to expose ourselves to contingency and fragility?

The Gospel is foolishness to the Jews because it says that *God's power* is revealed precisely in the agonizing death of a man on a cross. *What kind of sign is this?* we can imagine Paul's Jewish conversation partners asking. Don't we remember a God who smote the Egyptians with plagues and drowned them in the sea? How could a God revealed *through crucifixion* be a God with the power to save us from Rome? How can we trust a God with *this* kind of power?

The cross challenged the antique world's conceptions of *vulnerability*, *status*, and *power*. It said *no* to the flight from vulnerability, suggesting that sometimes risk-taking and suffering, especially with others, was the better course. It up-ended status hierarchies by pointing to a humiliating form of death reserved for *slaves* as a window on the character of God. And by declaring that divine power was evident in weakness, it brought into question the pyramidal organization of power in the ancient Mediterranean.

Much of Jesus' preaching and teaching focused on the issues of status, power, and vulnerability. His cleansing of the temple is a good example. It was a symbolic destruction of the focal point of Israel's religious and political life.

Many of Israel's leaders believed the nation's exile had been a divine judgment on their ancestors' spiritual compromises with their neighbors. Now that their nation had returned from captivity, they were determined to avoid such judgment in the future. That meant erecting cultural barriers between Israel and the rest of the world. The growing influence of Greco-Roman culture made it seem especially imperative that Israel define itself rigidly, excluding outsiders and preserving a stable identity.

Jesus' cleansing of the temple conveyed the message that rigid and exclusive concern for religious and national identity would ultimately lead to the annihilation of the temple and the religious and communal world it represented. A devotion to national spiritual status, a rejection of the vulnerability that might come from open intercourse with the outside world—these things would bring about the end of the temple and of Israel. As of course they did when Rome laid siege to Jerusalem four decades later.

The temple also symbolized the religious power of Israel's leaders, power that excluded the poor and the marginal, that preserved status and rejected vulnerability. Thus, Jesus' figurative destruction of the temple clearly expressed what he *said* when he taught justice and peace and what he *did* when he healed the excluded and welcomed outcasts to shared meals.

Problematic attitudes toward power, status, and vulnerability are evident not only in the ideology surrounding the temple but in a particular kind of commitment to *law*. In Judaism in the era of Paul and Jesus, the law was seen as God's special gift to Israel and a clear pointer to Israel's distinctiveness. Thus, the Book of Jubilees encourages a fidelity to law that entails exclusivism:

> Separate yourself from the Gentiles,
> > and do not eat with them,
> > > and do not perform deeds like theirs.
> And do not become associates of theirs.

> Because their deeds are defiled,
>> and all of their ways are contaminated,
>>> and despicable, and abominable.

Similar, the Letter of Aristeas declares that God "hedged . . . [the Jewish people] in on all sides with strict observances, . . . after the manner of the Law," in order "to prevent our being perverted by contact with others." The law served to underwrite claims of status and power and resist the vulnerability that might come from exposure to new ideas and different people and cultures.

It is notorious that law—perhaps especially *moral* and *religious* law—can be a means of maintaining power and status and avoiding vulnerability. Religious authorities can deploy law to establish their own legitimacy and suppress dissent. Law can be a means of marking boundaries, of identifying the bad people and separating them from the good people, and so preserving status. We can treat law an orderly blueprint for existence that eliminates surprise from our lives and helps to banish vulnerability.

This seems like a far cry from God's law as the psalmist sees it: perfect, enlightening, true, righteous, and worth desiring with passion. But if the Gospel *challenges* traditional conceptions of power, status, and vulnerability, and if law can be used to *support* those conceptions, how should we think about the notion of divine law today?

To begin with, the explicit precepts of the Ten Commandments embody a concern for the vulnerable. Prohibitions on murder, adultery, and theft can protect those with less power from those with more. The powerful are not to assert their invulnerability, preserve their status, maintain their authority by ignoring or riding roughshod over the weak.

This point is even clearer when we reflect on the relatively *generic* form of the commandments. As framed, they are addressed to *all* adult Israelite males: the same law applies across the board. To be sure, the Sabbath command assumes the reality of slavery, and women are not included—the command to covet refers explicitly to your neighbor's *wife*, not your neighbor's spouse. But the expansion of the moral community effected in later Judaism and in Christianity is a natural outgrowth of the simple principle that one law applies to all, even if "all" is still understood narrowly at the time of the Decalogue's original audience. This kind of generic law necessarily has an inclusive effect; because it applies consistently, without regard to status or role distinctions, it presupposes and fosters equality and resists hierarchies of status and power.

Also: the first two of the Ten Commandments prohibit idolatry. That is, they preclude our giving ultimate allegiance—the allegiance to which God alone is entitled—to any bit of finite reality. Of course that includes human organizations and possessions and nations. But it also includes human language, including language about goodness and justice—the language of law. Even the words we use to encapsulate God's call are *human* words. The first two commandments remind us that what we are called to do and be can never simply be identified with any human linguistic formulation. Any words we use are not *God* and not *God's words*.

That means that our moral judgments must always be destabilized by our recognition of the gap between ourselves and God. It means we can never proclaim God's judgment on others with smug self-confidence. It means we have to be open to new ways of thinking about God's call that allow us to be surprised by the voices we might be tempted to exclude. It means we can never rest content with the assumption that we possess of a tidy blueprint for human life that eliminates all the contingency, the fragility, the surprise.

Law is a metaphor. God is not a legislator, and what is good is not an arbitrary fiat of the divine *will*, as if God simply echoed the parent who says, "I'm your father, and you'll do what I tell you to do—or else!" What is good and right flows from the *nature of God's creation*. But the metaphor of law captures something important about the peremptory demand of requirements that are not subject to our whims and preferences. In particular, integral to the claim of goodness is centrally, unavoidably (even if not exclusively), the claim of human and non-human sentients that are different, that cannot be reduced to our categories or simply identified with ourselves or our interests. Thus, for instance, the prohibition on idolatry emphasizes that we cannot so absolutize our own perspectives (including our perspectives on goodness and justice and law) that we can no longer hear the voice of the other.

Contrary, then, to what we might initially think, the human language that is *law*, including the language of the Ten Commandments, can express insights apparent in Jesus' cleansing of the temple and Paul's proclamation of the foolishness of the cross. Understood as what it is—finite, fallible, human, but striving to embody God's goodness—the human language of law can help us protect the vulnerable, undercut unfair status claims, resist authoritarian power, and seek flourishing and fulfillment. Viewed this way, it truly has the potential to be a pointer to the shape goodness might take in our lives, a goodness more than, but encountered in and as, law—sweeter than honey, more desirable than gold.

44
What's Wrong with Wisdom?

"Wisdom" is hardly a dirty word for Jews, and it also wasn't for early Christians. And yet Paul seeks to challenge claims to wisdom. He seems, at minimum, to be confronting what he takes to be bad theology that issues, importantly, in bad practice. It is clear that the bad practice involves spiritual arrogance and self-aggrandizement. Perhaps this is at least part of what's going on, I think, in the critique of wisdom. The claim to possess insider knowledge that renders one spiritually superior and justifies domineering bossiness is disruptive and, ironically, foolish. The essence of idolatry is to identify one's own project (or some, any, human project, product, activity) with God's, as if human beings were capable (morally or intellectually) of representing God in any unqualified way. The person who claims to possess a special pipeline to divine truth, so that she or he is incapable of being corrected in light of the insights and experience and reflection of others, is unavoidably a troublemaker, and profoundly difficult to get along with. Consider the church leader who announces that, having prayed, he knows what God's will is with regard to some disputed matter, and that debate must cease so that his preferred approach can be pursued, or the political demagogue who claims that God is on the side of her or his nation, which can gleefully go to war against those who don't enjoy God's favor. (Paul himself sometimes seems to fall into this trap.)

Perhaps this, then, is Paul's primary point: that his opponents at Corinth claim that the special, revealed wisdom they possess immunizes them against critical challenge and entitles them to dominate the Corinthian congregation.

But I wonder if there's not another layer of meaning, too, which is suggested by some of what Paul says in and around the introduction to I Corinthians. Perhaps "wisdom" here might have suggested to some first-century readers rather the sort of thing the contemporary phrase "conventional wisdom" suggests to us. The conventional wisdom is the ordinarily accepted way of doing things, the way of seeing and responding to things embraced by the partisans of the *status quo*. Just watch any of the major news channels in the US and you'll see what conventional wisdom looks like.

We know something about the conventional wisdom of the ancient Mediterranean world. It embraced hierarchy and domination. It often treated those on the underside of history—women, children, slaves, losers—as if they deserved their fates. The notion that God could communicate to us through the story of a crucified man struck proponents of the conventional wisdom in the first-century world as absurd. Their view is captured in an ancient cartoon, one I'll mention again later in this book, that depicts a Christian worshipping a crucified man with the head of a donkey: weakness, failure, vulnerability—these couldn't possibly tell us anything fundamental about God.

Perhaps, then (we can only speculate), the domineering behavior of Paul's opponents in Corinth reflected not only their spiritual arrogance as presumed possessors of divine truth, but also their willingness to embrace the conventional wisdom of the ancient Mediterranean world, to see dominance and power as markers of divine favor. To try to control might be a predictable expression of this basic attitude. To challenge wisdom, then, would be to reject not just spiritual elitism but also, indirectly, the ordinary view of insiders and outsiders, the up and the down.

Seeing God's revelation in the life and death of a crucified criminal upended traditional ideas of power, dominance, and success, helping over the course of centuries to begin creating a place at the table in societies and cultures influenced by the Gospel for victims and the vulnerable. And it surely would have had this effect even without specific remembered teaching on Jesus' part. But in the versions of the Beatitudes contained Matthew's and Luke's gospels, early Christians preserved their memories of some of Jesus' most memorable and pithy aphorisms. Rejecting the association of goodness with excluding and subordinating the bad and the impure that preoccupied so many influential people in Israel in his day, Jesus called for and fostered an open, inclusive kind of community life. The early Church remembered him as underscoring the reality of an upside-down vision in which those dismissed as failures were seen as mattering, as loved and blessed by God, in which the merciful, rather than the hard-nosed and the hard-hearted, were commended, in which reconciliation trumped retaliation and retribution.

Jesus' teaching stood, of course, in the wake of both the prophetic tradition and the wisdom tradition. *Justice* in Micah 6 suggests both the correction of past injustice and the unwillingness to treat anyone as outside the moral community or as inherently less valuable. Humility need not, should not, mean self-loathing or self-despite or a refusal to accept honor, respect, and other good things—the point, rather, is that the humble person knows that the successes she or he enjoys do not change her or his fundamental moral standing, her or his equality in inherent value with everyone else. Everyone is God's creature. Everyone matters uniquely and irreplaceably. But no creature is absolute in value; no creature gets to pretend to be God, and to claim on this basis the right to dominate others or to treat them as if they, too, are not inherently worthwhile objects of respect and care.

The psalmist, too, calls for moral rectitude—for generosity, for loyalty, for the avoidance of injustice. Christians will rightly feel queasy at the thought, suggested by the psalmist's words, that the good person should despise anyone—we are all, again, God's children—but surely, at any rate, the good person does not praise unjust acts and is perfectly willing to critique them when doing so is appropriate. And, embracing the kind of rectitude spoken of by the psalmist (whether this is an implication the psalmist saw), we can emphasize that the vulnerable are just as valuable, just as worthwhile, as everyone else, not objects of scorn or derision nor people of whom advantage can rightly be taken.

The message that the vulnerable and the victims deserve a place at the table increasingly infiltrated Western consciousness as the story of Jesus began to spread. And, apart from virulent critics like Nietzsche, modern Westerners have tended to pay it lip-service. At the same time, we recognize that insider-outsider, up-down, pure-impure are categories with which contemporary people are all too familiar. Whether the issue is brutality in warfare which subjects dark-skinned foreigners to systematic cruelty that would be rejected out-of-hand if the targets were people like us, or an objectively racist criminal law that destroys families in minority communities and leaves enormous numbers of males in those communities in the custody of the legal system and thus permanently scarred and marginalized, or institutions that claim to represent God while, or even by, subordinating and excluding on the basis of gender—whether the issue is one of these inequities, or another, we still know the meaning of exclusion and subordination, of policies and procedures and institutions that deny the rights, undermine the dignity, silence the voices of victims and the vulnerable.

And so there is still reason for us to hear the psalmist's call for rectitude, the prophet's call for humility and mercy and justice, Paul's rejection of spiritual arrogance and the conventional wisdom of hierarchy, and Jesus' reminder that the peacemakers are blessed, and with them those who long for a wholeness they do not yet know and a brokenness of which they are continually reminded. May we know the unexpected, surprising blessing of which the Beatitudes speak and share it with those our lives touch in ways that turn conventional wisdom on its head.

45
Peace and Deliverance

For those who have undergone, or are undergoing, the kind of "great tribulation" experienced by the multitude in John's Apocalypse, no song could be sweeter than the song of peace. And in the midst of a seemingly endless war on an abstraction—"terror"—that provides excuses for torture, surveillance, and creeping authoritarianism, Jesus' blessing on the peacemakers couldn't be more timely. But it would also matter profoundly in quieter times.

The word "peace" has many associations, and some grander undertones, but I want to focus on its primary and most essential meaning: the absence of aggressive violence against people (and other sentients) and their justly acquired possessions. Peace in this sense is easy to ignore, easy to take for granted. But it is an absolutely vital requisite of civilized existence, and it is a natural expression of the recognition that each of us is an equally valuable child of God (as 1 John emphasizes).

Unfettered by the threat of aggression, people can cooperate voluntarily with each other, on their own terms. Peace enables us to form networks, potentially vast networks, of interdependence with the potential to contribute to flourishing and fulfillment across our planet. Peace as non-aggression may perhaps sometimes seem like a paltry thing when compared with a range of positive ideals, but it is in fact a crucial precondition for well being that can free people to work productively together and enable them to combine their ideas and exchange their resources in empowering and liberating ways, to decide for themselves how to craft relationships and institutions and build a better future. Peace matters.

The psalmist is confident that God will offer deliverance. And in the Apocalypse, God is praised as a God of "power and strength." Too often, we seem to expect a thoroughly muscular God to rescue us with decisive acts of unmistakable power—in the extreme, to make peace by making war. But John reminds us that the lamb praised by the multitude is a lamb whose blood has been spilled. Perhaps our most potent image of divine power is the picture of Jesus crucified, crying out, "My God, my God, why have you forsaken me?"

To incarnate God's *Logos*, God's Word, in the world is not to exercise absolute power. And, more broadly, God's will is all too frequently not done in the world. The God revealed in the crucified Jesus is not, it seems, a God who exercises the kind of coercive power required to overwhelm divine enemies with force. God, we may believe, is constantly at work to make peace in our world, to answer the cries of those who yearn for a liberating end to aggression. But the persuasive, rather than coercive, character of divine providence, the fact that God's action in the world is mediated action that takes place in and through the activities of creatures, means that the deliverance of peace cannot be expected to come in perfect, unambiguous fashion or as the product of a divine fiat that eliminates the freedom of creatures and the integrity of the physical world.

Also, too frequently, we seem to want God to make peace by humiliating or annihilating those we regard as the wicked. But the God we see revealed in Jesus, the Jesus who blesses the merciful, who urges the love of enemies, can hardly be expected to show mercy to us while mercilessly condemning our adversaries.

This hardly means that we should not try to stop injustice and secure recompense for its victims. It does mean, however, that we should not expect God to be a God of vengeance, just as we should ourselves decline to confuse defense against wrongdoing and the rectification of its effects with retaliation or retribution.

Those who call for peace may be persecuted like the prophets whose stories Jesus recalls. But let us remember how much what they do matters. The sharing of bread and wine symbolizes the unification of humanity through God's creation and healing grace. Ending aggression is a vital means of achieving this unification because it offers innumerable gifts: it enables people to share and trade and talk and travel and exchange and connect and recognize and depend upon and enrich each other. At Jesus' table, may we remember how precious the gifts of peace really are and reflect anew on the ways in which we can help God to wipe away the tears of those who mourn by giving these gifts to our world.

46
The Crucified Donkey

As I mentioned earlier, a kind of cartoon from the ancient Mediterranean world shows a man bowing before a crucified figure with the head of a donkey. The caption? "Alexamenos worships [his] God."

It is easy to imagine the guffaws of the onlookers who first observed this graffito. What kind of god would you ever expect to find on a cross, dying the death of a slave? It's hard to find an exact equivalent, but perhaps the image of a tattooed AIDS victim expiring in an electric chair might evoke the right sorts of feelings. A cross was no place for a god. Alexamenos must be a fool.

The soldiers who crucified Jesus saw the absurdity very clearly. The purple robe and the crown of thorns were pieces of demonic theater, designed to highlight just how bizarre it was that anyone should think that this captive, about to die the death Rome reserved for non-citizens who were common criminals, was a king.

For what is a king if not a ruler? And could Jesus of Nazareth be any less a ruler on the cross? He will have been, like the speaker in Psalm 22, the scorn of all his adversaries. Followers who had hoped to judge the nations at his side slunk away in fear or lingered at a distance from the cross in what they must have hoped was anonymity.

Among the most revelatory sentences in the entire Bible is the one quoted from this psalm that appears on the lips of Jesus in the narratives of the crucifixion in the First and Second Gospels: "My God, my God, why have you forsaken me?" For those who look to to the life of Jesus as a window on the identity and character of God, this sentence can seem utterly shocking. When we gaze at Jesus on the cross, we don't see power. We don't see a vengeful tyrant pronouncing judgment on the wicked. We don't see a cosmic administrator manipulating the details of history. We see a broken and agonized man screaming out in terror at the absence of God.

Vulnerability and Community

The window the cross provides on the nature of God helps to explain one of the most remarkable features of the Christ hymn Paul inserts in the middle of his letter to the Christians at Philippi. Jesus did not seek omnipotence, says the hymn. Instead, he submitted to death on a cross. *Therefore*, says the hymn, "God also highly exalted him...." *Therefore*.... Jesus' humiliation is the basis for his exaltation, its presupposition.

Paul's point in reciting the hymn is clear: the life of the Christian community is to embody a view of power modeled on the practice of Jesus. Inspired by compassion, the Philippian Christians are to seek solidarity with each other, unity, a graceful humility. This is just another way of saying that domination should be replaced by friendship, self-protective isolation by vulnerability.

His words are sufficiently familiar that we may find it hard to recognize in them the charter of a revolution. But they were. And are. The death of Jesus put to death inherited views of power and community. If we see God when we see the cross, then divine power, ultimate power, the power that matters most, must look very different from the power wielded by Herod or Tiberius Caesar. If the Messiah is the victim of this world's powers, then we must rethink our understanding of who victims really are.

Too often, communities define themselves by the people they exclude. They reject those who are different so that those who know they belong can feel superior in their belonging. Those who are rejected are expendable. Their loss and suffering are the price insiders pay for their own sense of self-worth.

The death of Jesus says an unmistakable *No!* to this view of community. We see it first, of course, in his own practice of teaching and healing and loving. Jesus willingly embraced his society's outsiders—the equivalents of today's AIDS victims, talk-show hosts, and undocumented workers. His teaching and the way he lived aroused opposition. But his response, though always strong, was never vengeful. Though he "set his face like a flint," he "gave his back to those who struck him and his cheeks to those who pulled out his beard." He absorbed the evil his opponents did to him, and in so doing unmasked it.

Vulnerability and Community

His death makes the point even more clearly. The good people in Jesus' society, the ones who stood for purity and righteousness, showed what a commitment to purity and righteousness *as ends in themselves* can lead to. They put on display the consequences of boundary maintenance and exclusion. When they hung him on the cross, they highlighted the bankruptcy of the entire system of scapegoating and victimization.

Suppose we were to accept a view of power according to which vulnerability is divine. Suppose that, with Jesus, our communities said *No!* to the blame game—refusing to victimize and exclude those who are different to make ourselves feel better?

The result would be a new kind of communal practice in our churches, our families, our workplaces. To hear the gospel of the cross as a gospel of inclusive community, a gospel with a new view of vulnerable power, would mean many things.

It would mean listening, truly listening, to the fears, the hopes, and the dreams of our ideological opponents. We may be so sure about law, or economics, or gender equality, or the gifts of the Spirit, or salvation, or a million and one other things that we fail to acknowledge and cherish the personhood of our opponents, whatever the nature of our disagreements with them.

It would mean reaching out across generational lines, to understand why our parents fear for us the way they do, why our children resent the signs that we are out of touch—refusing to answer the question, *Why?* with sullen disregard or invulnerable authority.

It would mean opening our hearts and homes and pews and workplaces and pulpits to the people who don't fit in: people who aren't like us ethnically, religiously, socioeconomically, culturally, sexually, ideologically. It would mean refusing to say to anyone, simply because he or she was different, "You don't belong here!" It would mean resisting the urge to turn anyone into a scapegoat, to shore up our faltering sense of self by demeaning anyone else. It would mean abandoning the categories we use to organize our emotional and domestic and social and ecclesial and ideological worlds around the insider-outsider distinction.

Each of us has a different story. What living out the gospel of the cross in the course of our individual stories will look like isn't something I can describe usefully at a high level of abstraction. I do know this, though: taking the gospel seriously will mean recalling repeatedly that divine power is the power of a God who suffers rather than dominating, refusing to deny or evade the reality of vulnerability and risk, continually opening ourselves to all the small and large deaths that inviting love into our lives may render inescapable. And it will mean recalling repeatedly that the cross as Christians remember it reveals with striking clarity the results of attempting to define the boundaries between insiders and outsiders. The gospel calls us to say no to domination and yes to vulnerability. It calls us to say no to victimization, and yes to hospitality. It calls us to learn from the story of Jesus in ways that enable a new world to happen in our midst.

47
On Being a Victim

A college contemporary of mine, whom I'll call Chris, is a victim. Family pathology and physical trauma have both taken their toll. "Why has God done this to me?" is a question to which I've struggled to respond. I've tried to reason with Chris: God doesn't want you to suffer. God doesn't intend for you to hurt. But what I've realized over time is that, for Chris, the belief that God is responsible is curiously comforting. It implies that there is order and meaning in what might otherwise seem like pointless misery. Everything happens for a *purpose*. And, perhaps even more importantly, there's somebody to blame.

But understanding our lives in this way is incompatible with the Gospel. The Christian message undercuts both a cheery optimism that sees a divine plan behind every calamity, and a perverse passivity that finds strength in the moral superiority that comes from being able to blame God. The Gospel is not a means of escape. Its purpose is not to confer on us an unruffled security. It is not a passport beyond the ravages of change and chance, confusion and chaos, degeneration and death. It calls us to own the reality of an enveloping darkness, not to deny it or to seek fruitlessly to elude it.

The biblical witness clearly acknowledges the obscurity that surrounds us—not as the whole of the story, but as an inescapable part of it. "My God, my God, why have you forsaken me?" cries the psalmist. "O my God, I cry by day, but you do not answer; and by night, but find no rest." "Oh, that I knew where I might find him," the biblical Job is depicted as yearning. In passages like these, the biblical writers squarely face the reality that God's absence haunts us in times of desolation.

The biblical writers' awareness of helplessness and frustration highlight for us the reality that the person of faith is not immunized against these aspects of the human condition. Especially revealing is the story of Jesus. The Gospels recall Jesus as quoting the words of Psalm 22 from the cross: "My God, my God, why have you forsaken me?" We cannot comfort ourselves with the utterly unwarranted notion that this was simply a piece of play-acting. Here we see Jesus utterly desolate, utterly abandoned, utterly alone with the suffering that overwhelms him. And so, in turn, if we can see God in Jesus, we can be prompted to discern that God suffers this same abandonment, this same loss, this same frustration, this same forsakenness. When Jesus' project is rejected, God's project is rejected. When Jesus' character provokes opposition, God's character is the ultimate object of the assault.

If God suffers the brokenness and isolation that Jesus suffers, if Jesus is not exempt from the obscurity and confusion that dog our steps, then we cannot find in the gospel any license for some sort of holy escapism. Our "great high priest . . . in every respect has been tested as we are." This is a source of confidence, to be sure, but it is not confidence that we will be able to elude the tests we face repeatedly as human beings. It is confidence that God is with us whatever happens.

Christians must affirm, in Nicholas Lash's words, "that the world has meaning and purpose." But they must also accept "with full seriousness the implication of the claim . . . that the paradigm of divine action in the world is the passion of the Lord's anointed." And so they must be skeptical of claims "that this meaning and purpose may—whether in respect of particular events or of large-scale patterns in human history—be straightforwardly . . . 'read off' our individual or group experience." God's power is not the power of coercive control but the power of persuasive love. This kind of power is vulnerable power, power that, while never defeated, is always constrained, always dependent on the free choices of creatures and the behavior of physical and biological systems. It is power that offers no guarantees except the guarantee of a never-ending, always loving divine presence. In choosing to create a world rather than to stage a puppet show, God has chosen to live without control. That is why Jesus must cry, "My God, my God, why have you forsaken me?," why the person of faith is not exempt from pain and darkness.

Vulnerability and Community

To live in a world undergirded by *this* kind of power is to relinquish the demand that God order the world to meet our whims. It is to let go of the opportunity to blame God, however comforting it might be to do so. And it is in turn to model our own action on God's. Thus, it is to relinquish the insistence that we be in control. Control is a temptation not because we somehow do not deserve secure, manageable lives, but because our own capacities are always limited, because we *cannot* really manage reality as we would like. And this is one of the many lessons contained in the always unsettling story of the man we often call "the rich, young ruler."

What, he asks, must he do to be part of what God is doing in Jesus for the renewal of Israel? How can he be part of God's project? Jesus calls him to abandon his source of security, his means of control, his means (as Dick Winn notes) of *doing good*, and come to the party! It may be that, as André Trocmé suggests, Jesus asked of his followers that they enact among themselves something like the Levitical Year of Jubilee, with its cancellation of debts and return of ancestral property. Hey may have called all of Israel to let go of a traditional attachment to land that was part of an oppressive identity politics paving the way for confrontation with Rome—and still very much alive in today's Middle East. Whatever its rationale, challenging property claims is unavoidably caught up with challenging our illusory security.

It is crucial to emphasize again that there is nothing wrong with being, or with wanting to be, secure. We need security. Change can be terrifying. Unpredictability can rob us of confidence. But the struggle for security can lead us to trample on intransigent reality, to crush whatever gets in the way of our safety. And achieving a modicum of security can foster the illusion that we really are in charge of our own destiny, that we really can banish chance and disease and death. The result is an absurd and destructive spiritual arrogance.

Note what follows the story of the rich young man in Mark 10. After his sorrowing departure, the disciples again hear Jesus announce his impending death in verses 32 and 33. And Jesus rejects James and John's identification of his project with monarchical authority in verses 35-45. The evangelist sets the story in the context of Jesus' progress toward Jerusalem and toward his Passion. The young man refuses dispossession. But Jesus makes clear that he anticipates the ultimate dispossession—death—at Passover time. And he urges his disciples to let go of dreams of kingly power—encouraging them not to see their role in his future realm as one marked by possessive control.

The Gospel is not the good news of clarity and security. It is not the good news of a divine plan that absolves us of responsibility, or of a divine wisdom that banishes doubt. It is the good news that we do not have to be God. Except that that's the wrong way to put it, since it implies that God is in the control business, a notion that should be thoroughly difficult to maintain for anyone who sees God revealed on the cross. We do not have to emulate the sorts of deities we sometimes wish were there to worship: manipulative controllers. We can rest in the confidence to which Hebrews 4 refers, the confidence that comes from grace, even when we don't or can't successfully manage the history of the world. The gospel is the good news that, in spite of the unavoidable consequences of living in as finite and fallible persons in a world whose order and chaos sometimes seem to conspire against us, we live in the midst of a divine love that has experienced and continues to experience the horror, the violence, the loss that come from living without control. The gospel is the good news that God is with us.

48
Everybody Suffers

Everybody suffers. To suffer is, at root, to allow, to permit—to be passive. We suffer when we are not in complete control of our lives, when we are subjected to forces that lie outside our control. And this means, in turn, that suffering is endemic to—indeed, constitutive of—the human condition. For we are all constantly and unavoidably subject to the influences of innumerable forces beyond our control. Suffering is an unavoidable concomitant of finite existence; finite realities cannot so master their environments that they can control all things and eliminate chance, contingency, and conflicts of interest. There is, in this sense, no life without suffering.

This isn't intended to deny the obvious fact that some suffering isn't, and some is, accompanied or signaled by severe pain—what we often think of when we use the word "suffering." Nor does it mean, of course, that the quality and significance of everyone's suffering is identical.

The distinction is evident in 1 Peter. Addressing Christian slaves, the epistle observes that "it is commendable if a person bears up under the pain of *unjust* suffering," while maintaining that it is nothing to be proud of if one "receive[s] a beating for doing *wrong* and endure[s] it." We rightly wince at the argument, which presupposes that slave masters—like the kings and governors to whom the epistle has referred earlier, and the patriarchal husbands to whom it will turn next—exercise their power legitimately, and that one could thus suffer *justly* for disobeying them. But it is with some relief that we note that this disquisition on the putative obligations of slaves serves almost as an excuse for a meditation of more lasting value—a meditation on the sufferings of Jesus.

Jesus is presented here as the paradigmatic innocent sufferer. He is innocent not only in that he did not deserve the cruel abuses to which he was subjected—as if anyone could deserve such abuses—

but also in that he maintained a stance of generosity and grace even throughout his Passion. Refusing to threaten retaliation, "he entrusted himself to [God,] who judges justly."

Paradoxically, says 1 Peter, it is by Jesus' *wounds* that the epistle's readers "have been *healed*." In what does this healing consist? "For you were like sheep going astray, but now you have returned to the Shepherd and Overseer of your souls."

Note the language of *return* here. God is where we belong. God is where we are at home. To find ourselves anew in God is not to enter some alien realm; it is, instead, to realize ourselves at home. If God is our home, we cannot ever really leave, for God is everywhere and always with us. But we can be more or less aware of and responsive to the reality that we are at home in God.

First Peter is concerned throughout with the suffering of the first-century Christian community; the epistle returns more than once to this theme in other contexts. So I would not wish to suggest that the author or the original audience would have sought to elucidate the idea of return and the idea of suffering in relation to each other in just the way in which I should like to do so. But I think there's something provocative and helpful about reading the talk of suffering and homecoming together, in light of the story of Jesus.

While they have employed diverse concepts and images for this purpose, Christians from the first century to the present have persistently spoken of the human story of Jesus of Nazareth as *iconic*, of Jesus' humanity as a medium through which God's glory could be displayed. And that glory has, in turn, been understood as inseparable from Jesus' suffering. Christians have frequently seen Jesus' suffering as a pointer to the reality of God's suffering with us at every moment of our existence.

This, then, is one thing it means to see God as our home. If we are at home with and in God, we can and should say not only that *we* belong with God, as we do, but also that *God* belongs with us, where we are. And where we are there is suffering. To come home to God—which is to say, to know ourselves always already at home with God—is not, therefore, to escape to some realm free of suffering. There can be no such realm, if suffering is part of finite existence. Rather, to come home to God is in part to recognize that, precisely in our suffering, we are accompanied, and cherished, by a God who suffers with us.

Consider Psalm 23. Its original readers may well have heard in the psalmist's words a confession that God's providential power provided insurance against loss and enmity and a guarantee of access to various human goods—to a winning ticket in the lottery of life. It is hard to say. It is understandable that they might have focused on these things: life in ancient Israel was often hard; temporal, sensory needs are insistent; and there was little or no expectation of life beyond death. But we cannot comfortably adopt a similar focus. We see too much pain and loss, in our own lives and in the lives of others, to entertain any illusion that God's good will is always done, that we can be free from suffering in a world marked by finitude, fallibility, freedom, and sin. We know that God's influence on the world is persuasive, not coercive, and that creatures say not only *yes* but also *no* to divine persuasion.

But we can see another layer of meaning in the psalm, I think. We can see it as a testament to the activity of a God whose presence can sustain us even as we confront our enemies or traverse the valley of the shadow of death. We can see God as suffering with us, then, even when we are subjected to the unjust authority of kings, slave masters, and patriarchal husbands—and even when that suffering is legitimated and intensified by being described as God's will (for is not our suffering worse when we are told that we deserve it?), when it is undergirded by appeals to passages like those found in 1 Peter 2 and 3. We can confess that God is with us at these times—at work, to be sure, for concrete improvements in our empirical circumstances, but loving us and suffering with us *even* when these improvements do not come about. So God is our shepherd, in the sense suggested by Psalm 23 and 1 Peter alike, precisely by *being with* us—and that means, in turn, by *suffering* with us.

Jesus' suffering can be seen as redemptive, as 1 Peter suggests. But this is not because pain is a good thing in and of itself. It is not because pain is expiatory, as if my pain and loss could make up for someone else's. Rather, it is because it can be seen as pointing us toward the pain, toward the suffering, of a God who is *Emmanuel*, God with us. God who is our shepherd is, as I have already noted that Whitehead wrote, "the fellow-sufferer who understands." While God is passionately concerned about and responsive to the empirical circumstances of our lives, the nature of divine influence on the world means that God's will is regularly flouted. Even when it is, however, even when we suffer pain and loss, we can know that who we are is rooted in God, that meaning of our lives transcends our fluctuating empirical circumstances, and that we can anticipate a future *in God* even when all seems lost. It is in this sense that we can confess that God is the "good shepherd," that, even in the valley of the shadow of death, we truly need fear no evil.

49
Binding Up the Body

As the Fourth Gospel tells the story, Joseph of Arimathea carefully arranges to take custody of Jesus' body. And then he and Nicodemus prepare it for burial.

This is an interesting image. Both are wealthy. It would be reasonable to expect each to involve retinues of servants. But the picture in John 19 is of "the two of them" personally wrapping the body.

We can see this as a reflection of both a desire for safety and a personal attachment to Jesus. It's not clear that making large numbers of people aware of one's support for a man just executed as a terrorist by the Roman government would have been conducive to good health in first-century Palestine. But I think John also wants us to think of Joseph and Nicodemus as people who want to take personal responsibility for his body, who want to care for him now, at the last.

They had not done so earlier, John says: Joseph "feared the Jews." John uses "the Jews" as a pejorative on many occasions. But since Joseph, and Nicodemus, and the disciples—and, of course, Jesus himself—were all Jewish, it's apparent that "the Jews" doesn't mean "all Jews." Perhaps it is synonymous with "the leadership of Israel at the time of Jesus" or "the establishment," much as we sometimes hear people say that "Americans" do this or that, or, even worse, that "we" do this or that, when the reference is obviously not to all Americans, or even most, but rather to foolish or criminal people exercising coercive power in the name of the American people. Or perhaps the Fourth Gospel's perspective is that "the real Jews" are those who opposed Jesus and that people, even of Jewish ancestry, who identify with Jesus are part of the new Israel, and therefore not really part of the old.

It's not clear. What is clear, though, is that Joseph has been afraid of political reprisals; we must assume that the same is true of Nicodemus.

One of the great myths of modern, popular Christianity seems to be that Jesus spent a year—or, as in the account we find in the Fourth

Gospel, three years—wandering the countryside preaching niceness only to get himself executed for his pains. (A slightly different version has him trying to provoke an execution in order to appease a retributively minded God.) I think it is clear that the real Jesus was a troublemaker, one who caused a great deal of anger and frustration on the part of many of his contemporaries.

This seems to have been because he practically embodied a powerful vision of inclusive community, one that didn't exclude women, poor people, social outcastes, tax collectors, people who collaborated with an oppressive occupying power—even the hated Romans themselves. In place of a community maintained by clearly demarcating insiders and outsiders, Jesus called for, and put on display, a kind of community in which the welcome table was spread for everyone.

If you don't believe doing that can make you a target of violence, consider the story of Clarence Jordan, whose Koinonia Farms, which was located in rural Georgia before the Civil Rights era and which became a model of interracial solidarity, was the focus of intense, vitriolic opposition—just because it put a different kind of world on display.

Jesus was *persona non grata* as far as those in power were concerned, so it's easy to see why people like Nicodemus and Joseph might have been disinclined to identify with him publicly. Conflict is stressful. So is upsetting the establishment.

It's no fun to be excluded, to be left out, to be ridiculed and dismissed. And, as Jesus' own fate reminds us, his followers risked more than just not being invited to the best parties. We might choose self-righteously to condemn those who shunned confrontation. And we might wonder whether the famous commentator Matthew Henry was quite right to treat standing up for Jesus after his death as somehow a *greater* expression of faithfulness than standing up for him during his lifetime. But not everyone can or should take a stand for every cause all the time. And, indeed, the Gospels treat Nicodemus's presence "on the inside," made possible by his discretion, as perhaps working to Jesus' advantage on occasion.

In any event, whether we conclude that people like Nicodemus and Joseph should have shown more courage or not, we find them here, now, taking responsibility for Jesus' body. To the extent that we think that what they did was good for Jesus, as the story's original readers certainly would have thought, we cannot but be struck by the psalmist's call for divine deliverance. The psalmist sees God as a "rock of refuge," "a strong fortress." But at this point, God's grace is manifested not in deeds of power but in the gentle, intimate care of two men seeking to avoid the gaze of the authorities and taking personal responsibility for preparing Jesus' corpse for burial.

Easter is a celebration of hope. The Easter story is a grand one, naturally told to the accompaniment of trumpet fanfares. But in this story, on Easter Sabbath, the tones are muted. Here, in the dark night, as hope seems to have died with Jesus on the cross, and the disciples, like Jesus, are inclined to cry out, "My God, my God, why have you forsaken me?," God's grace is quietly work in the gentle hands of two men who have feared reprisals for making their loyalty to Jesus public but who now, when all of the others who have loved Jesus are hiding in the shadows, step forward to embrace his broken body.

Divine providence is not marked by trumpet blasts and the deafening voices of angel choirs. God does not always work in the dramatic, the powerful, the overwhelming. God's power is evident, as Paul reminds us, in weakness. Here, in the ministry of the fearful, that power is surprisingly revealed.

While we have not witnessed dramatic irruptions of divine power, accompanied by the blaring of brass instruments and flashes of celestial light; but we may have seen—we may, indeed, have been—*instances* of God's providence gently at work amidst emptiness and brokenness, like the fearful Nicodemus and Joseph, binding up Jesus' body for burial.

50
The End of Sacrifice

Sometimes it's hard to hold a group of people together. Rivalry and competing desires can be fertile breeding grounds for violence. Over time, though, as René Girard has emphasized, people have found one especially powerful way of defusing violence.

Sacrifice.

A group whose members are on the verge of killing each other can redirect their rage at a scapegoat—a person or a thing that becomes a new focus for their violence. Instead of taking out their hatred on each other, they can target someone or something else. The scapegoat may be an outsider, a member of the community who is converted into an outsider to make her or him a convenient sacrifice. Either way, sacrificing the scapegoat can keep people from killing each other.

More than that, it can bind them together. Uniting to destroy someone else, people find a new sense of common purpose and common identity. Scapegoating is a wonderful way for those who do the scapegoating to bond, as they unite in a violent ritual that takes away their felt need to kill each other.

When societies select their sacrificial victims, they draw a clear dividing line between those who sacrifice on the one hand and their victims on the other. Sacrifice thus presupposes a self-righteous distinction between those who sacrifice and those who are sacrificed. And because they are supposed to purify the sacrificers or satisfy the gods or reestablish cosmic harmony, they reinforce the sense on the part of the sacrificers that they are in the right.

Sacrifices can be tremendously powerful: they hold societies together and keep the awesome power of violence at bay. So it's hardly surprising that myths of sacrifice figure prominently in the world's religious traditions. Human and animal sacrifice figure in the biblical traditions, to be sure. And yet sacrifice provokes tension, a tension that explodes with the story of Jesus.

The story of Abraham and Isaac on Mount Carmel helps to effect a dramatic transition in our cultural history. It depicts what we can see as the recognition that God is not in the human sacrifice business. It both prompts and reflects the increasing realization that, despite the seeming power of human sacrifice to relieve our feelings of guilt, bind us together, and give us a sense of security, it can't ultimately deliver what it seems to promise.

The promise is simple: Violence against someone else can purify us, establish our moral rectitude. We can displace our evil onto someone or something else. We can water our societies with blood.

The story of Jesus says an unequivocal *no* to the idea of the sacrificial scapegoat. It is better that one man should die for the people than that the whole nation should perish, Caiaphas asserts in the Fourth Gospel. And so untrammeled power sets out to identify and destroy another victim, just as it has done so often in the past. But the readers of the gospel who hear Caiaphas's words know that this victim is innocent if any victim is innocent. And so they also know that the whole system of victimization and sacrifice is suspect. The death of Jesus starkly places a question mark next to the practice of sacrificial scapegoating on which societies routinely rely to maintain their stability and their identities.

Though the biblical story can be read as, among other things, a story of humanity's liberation from the perverse logic of human sacrifice, it is not a story in which everyone gets the point immediately. Take a story from Exodus. According to the story, in the shadow of Sinai, the people of Israel lapse into sacrificial rituals centering around an idol representing a fertility god during Moses' absence. Traditional sacrificial rituals still exert power over their imaginations. The Exodus story, retold in the book of Psalms, features Moses' touching plea for Israel. Ironically, however, in the biblical narrative, he responds to Israel's relapse into traditional sacrificial ritual practice by unleashing on his return to the Israelite camp an orgy of what amounts to human sacrifice, turning the clan of Levi loose, with swords drawn, on their cousins until the camp overflows with blood. It is hard to escape the logic of sacrifice, the sense that order will be restored and purity regained if only the outsider, the person on the other side, falls on the sacrificial altar.

Not every story in the Bible is edifying in the sense that it presents a model for us to copy. The story of Jesus reveals the indefensibility of sacrificial violence by challenging us to see things from the perspective of the victim. Moses' great compassion prefigures that of Jesus; but his willingness to strike down his fellow Israelites points out just how strong is the hold the idea of violence as purification and communal bonding exerts on our imaginations.

The spiral of violence prompts the people in Jesus' parable of the wedding feast to kill the king's servants who invite them to come to a wedding party. And it prompts the king to behave as kings so often do: to respond with violence and destroy his ungrateful subjects. Those the king has invited to the party assert their power and express their contempt for the king through violence. And the king, in turn, meets their violence with implacable violence of his own.

We should not expect to find the king a perfect image of God in this parable, any more than the characters' in Jesus' other parables should be seen as providing flawless models of God (or humanity). Jesus describes not the character of God but the all-too-familiar character of humanity in the behavior of the king and the wedding guests alike. Both are petty: surely it makes no sense to respond to a wedding invitation with violence, nor to kill those who choose not to accept the invitation. And both are unable to escape the cycle of sacrificial violence. The king has prepared for the wedding feast by killing animals, but responds to the ingratitude of the invitees by sacrificing them, too.

The king prepares for the wedding of his son with murder. But Jesus, as the readers of the gospel would have known, is himself the murdered. The innocent victim, he prays: Father, forgive them . . . . Jesus' own behavior contrasts sharply with that of the king in the parable. Jesus breaks the cycle of sacrificial violence.

The message that the sacrificial system results in the death of God's anointed, that the victim is innocent and the sacrificers guilty not in spite of but because of their sacrifice, undergirds a commitment to reconciliation. The barriers between victims and victimizers are broken down. Who is in the right and who in the wrong ceases to be a justification for exclusionary violence, for community-maintaining violence, for identity- and ego-sustaining violence—for sacrifice.

Thus, Paul appeals for reconciliation, not for scapegoating violence, calling upon two women who have worked closely with him to come into renewed relation with each other. And in words that have become famous, he exhorts: ". . . whatsoever things are true, whatsoever things are honest, whatsoever things are just, whatsoever things are pure, whatsoever things are lovely, whatsoever things are of good report; if there be any virtue, and if there be any praise, think on these things."

What, in light of this injunction, are we to say of the Bible's stories of sacrificial violence? What could make such stories just and pure and lovely? To emulate them is to reject the gospel. There may be (I think there is) a place in the Christian life for regretfully defending oneself and others against aggression by force. But there is certainly no place in the Christian life for the use of pointless and self-righteous sacrificial violence, violence that rejects and excludes and preserves a dubious sense of moral superiority and community cohesion. So the Christian cannot call for an orgy of bloodshed because people worship idols or reject the good news. Precisely in light of the gospel, however, another meaning emerges. The character of God is more clearly seen in Moses' plea for Israel than in his command to the Levites to deal death to their cousins. God's realm may be a lot like a wedding party, but God isn't a lot like a petulant tyrant. The Gospel is the good news of reconciliation. It is the good news that the barriers between victims and victimizers can and must be broken down. It is the good news that we can find our identities in God's love, not in violence.

It is the end of sacrifice.

Part V
Passion and Delight

51
"I Want Never Got"

According to a barbed piece of advice offered to British children of a previous generation, "*I want* never got." Expressing your desire was rude, whiny—and a sure way to avoid getting what you wanted. In fact, the best way to prepare children for the rigors of the so-called "real world" was to say *no* to anything they seemed to want very much. Children raised this way soon discover that desire is a bad idea.

Even American children whose parents have never told them wanting was a bad idea can learn to shun desire. A child gets the message readily enough: if she lets mom and dad know just how intensely she really values something, parents who want to control her behavior will refuse to give her what she desires or, if it's already hers, take it away. The more passionately she desires, the more vulnerable she is to pain and loss. She discovers that not wanting anything very much is a great way to stay safe and pain-free. So she comes to associate desire with deprivation, and therefore to avoid it.

So it can come as a bit of a shock to read Psalm 63. "[M]y soul thirsts for you," the psalmist says to God. "[M]y body longs for you." "[Y]our love is better than life." The language is unabashedly erotic; the psalmist yearns for God with all the passion of a lover. The prophetic word in Isaiah 55 begins on a similar note. Our need for God is like thirst. God's faithful, covenantal love slakes this thirst like wine or milk. The food God offers is "the richest of fare." It evokes "delight." The use of such powerful sensual imagery seems to imply that the love of God answers to human desire.

It's difficult to read passages like this and still suppose that all desire is bad. They assume that passion is an inescapable and appropriate part of life. But perhaps even if passion is OK, someone might imagine, only God deserves our passionate devotion. Maybe we ought to desire deeply, but only if our desire focuses on God. Only God won't disappoint us, abuse our vulnerability, take advantage of our devotion to manipulate and dominate us. And maybe the very intensity of our passion means we should direct it toward God alone because only God is beautiful and wonderful enough to deserve truly intense love.

It wouldn't be difficult to find this sort of approach echoed in a lot of Christian piety. But the notion that only God is worthy of passion runs up against a crucial Christian belief: that God responds to *us* with passion. God desires us. God goes in search of us. It's not because we're safe to love; no one who sees God revealed in the image of Jesus hanging on the cross should suppose that God opts for security over vulnerability. We disappoint and reject God perennially, but, the Gospel affirms, divine love continues to woo us.

God suffers. God is passionate. So our own passion is part of what it means to be made in God's image. And the world is God's good work. If God's creativity lies behind our world, there seems to be something wrong with the notion that what God most wants from us is to turn away from that world, to escape from it by turning our desires toward God alone. If the world is God's good work, then it ought to be worth desiring—particularly given that, as Christians confess, God desires union with creation.

The passionate desire of psalmist and prophet is a response to God's creation and a reflection of God's own passion. Why, then, have so many Christians, so many people who have sought to be spiritually vital, been suspicious of passion? Are there any reasons other than the simple fear of vulnerability?

One reason, a good one, is the fear of narcissism. The desire to connect with others, to be acknowledged and desired by them, can become all consuming. We can too easily see others only in relation to ourselves, as if they simply orbited around us. The parent who thinks of a child primarily as a source of affirmation may be passionate, just like the would-be lover who interprets the beloved's distance as a reflection on himself because he cannot acknowledge the other challenges that consume her. But neither truly loves, despite how loving she or he may *feel*.

Another reason passion might seem to be problematic is its tendency to reflect and encourage the demand that its object deliver more than any human person, institution, or community *can* deliver.

No individual or group can offer us ultimate fulfillment; and to ask for it is both to bring about one's own certain disappointment and to tempt oneself to seek to control the other so one will be more likely to experience the satisfaction one seeks.

But the problem here is *neither* that one desires *nor* that one desires some finite reality rather than God. The problem is that one fails to temper the love that is desire with another kind of love, love that sees the other truly as *other* than oneself and that sees both self and other in relation to God. This kind of love acknowledges that one is a creature, finite, limited, and not the center of the universe. The truth about God's good world calls us not to abandon desire but to love aright, to abandon narcissistic or idolatrous desire in favor of a desire that sees finite things as valuable, worthy of our desire and care, as parts of God's *good* creation, but which also sees them *as finite*, limited, incomplete—that sees them as *parts* of God's good creation. To love in this way is to *repent*.

Disciplining desire is one way to heed the warnings from Israel's history which Paul elaborates in the Corinthian correspondence. The disciplined heart shuns idolatry, because it acknowledges that creatures are loveable without treating any finite thing as a satisfactorily ultimate ground of meaning and hope. The disciplined heart shuns sexual exploitation, because it respects others as *others* and refuses to deceive or manipulate or betray them. Disciplining desire is also a way to attend to the call to repentance Jesus is remembered as issuing in Luke 13.

The focus in this passage is not on repentance in general. It is rather on the abandonment of a particular kind of desire, an idolatrous desire for an absolutely secure national identity. Unless Israel turned away from the idea that it had to maintain its identity by rejecting outsiders and building high walls that separated it from the impure and the foreign, Jesus foresaw that Roman might would topple Jerusalem to the ground. There is nothing wrong with love of place. But there is something wrong with a desire for a secure national identity that can be purchased only at the price of excluding and marginalizing and rejecting those who are different.

The challenge for Jesus' contemporaries was, as it is for us, the challenge to love aright—to care deeply and passionately for people and places and institutions without lapsing into narcissism or idolatry. To love rightly, to discipline desire, is not to repress feeling or abandon love for some kind of tight-lipped moralism. It is to love creation as God loves it—intensely and vulnerably, but with the awareness that it is not God. Disciplined desire respects God's creation for what it is. It reaches out to God's world with God's own passion.

52
Seven Years

Seven years. Jacob works for seven years for the privilege of receiving Laban's blessing on his marriage to Rachel. He has something to look forward to—the chance to marry the woman he loves. And so he is quite willing to postpone gratification. In the Genesis story, he clearly judges that Rachel is worth it. He adores her, and, as a result, the seven years of toil for Laban "seem[] like only a few days to him because of his love for her." And even when Laban deceives him, he nonetheless chooses to wait for the one he desires and delights in and cares for.

Who knows whether Rachel would have prompted a similar reaction on anyone else's part? She didn't need to. What matters is that Jacob loves her—a fact his labor for seems likely to have deepened. As St.-Exupery's Little Prince says to the many roses that are not the special one he has tended: "You are beautiful, but you are empty. One could not die for you. To be sure, an ordinary passerby would think that my rose looked just like you—the rose that belongs to me. But in herself alone she is more important than all the hundreds of you other roses: because it is she that I have watered; because it is she that I have put under the glass globe; because it is she that I have sheltered behind the screen; . . . because it is she that I have listened to, when she grumbled, or boasted, or even sometimes when she said nothing. Because she is my rose." Jacob has worked for seven years for Rachel; she is his rose (or gardenia, or frangipani).

Empowering and inspiring us as it does to meet and overcome challenges like the one Jacob confronted, love is remarkable. Too often, of course, we fumble, marring our loves with impatience or blindness or fickleness or jealousy or superficiality or sloth or a penchant for control. And so it is hardly surprising that a story like this one, a story of determination and faithfulness and devotion, has the capacity to move us. We want to know that love like this is possible. We want to love like this ourselves, and to be loved like this ourselves.

The kind of committed devotion Jacob exhibits in this story can be seen as a representation of the sort of faithful, reliable divine love which the psalmist affirms—"He remembers his covenant forever"—and about which Paul writes in Romans 8; as a means by which that love is mediated to us; and as a way in which we respond rightly to the God who love us in this way.

"Who shall separate us from the love of Christ?," Paul asks. "I am convinced," he says in response "that neither death nor life, neither angels nor demons, neither the present nor the future, nor any powers, neither height nor depth, nor anything else in all creation, will be able to separate us from the love of God that is in Christ Jesus our Lord." I suspect he is primarily concerned with love as the ground of our ultimate hope. He wants to say, I think, that he is confident in virtue of God's love that we can hope for a personal future with God beyond death. And yet he speaks more broadly, emphasizing the persistent availability of that love.

When we pray the Lord's Prayer and say, "Thy will be done," we are reminded that this is *a prayer* precisely because the goodness God seeks is so often is *not* achieved; there would be no point to the prayer if things were otherwise. God's goodness is realized in the world, when it is, not unilaterally, not by means of divine coercion—we would live in a very different kind of world if it were—but through mutual interaction, persuasion. God works in the world in and through what God has made. But creatures are real, not divine puppets, and they much too frequently don't do what God intends. Freedom and fallibility and ignorance and sin combine to ensure that humans and other creatures often fail, sometimes quite spectacularly, to realize God's intentions in their own lives and the lives of others. Individuals, whole societies, whole traditions, fail to catch what God seeks to convey to them about important matters, fail to respond aptly to divine persuasion at crucial times.

And that is certainly true of how we love. We are all too often not loved well. We all to often do not love well. At root, we are capable of love, social, able to give and receive delight and desire and care. But fear and the impulse to escape insecurity by controlling and the inability to escape family scripts and a thousand and one losses and wounds and a cascade of other liabilities hamper our capacity to do so. Our love is not perfect.

But it is not for that reason unreal. Lovers, friends, parents, children—all manage, fitfully, imperfectly, but genuinely to touch each other's lives with healing and hope, pleasure and joy, wonder and comfort.

So human love, with all its imperfections, can, indeed, be a crucial way in which we know God's love. Our picture of divine love is shaped, like all our pictures of God, by our human experience, with the result that our experience provides the template through which we interpret what talk of divine love means. But it's not just a matter of interpretation and understanding: God loves in and through the love we receive and the love we give (and this is true, of course, whether we recognize it or not—love given and received matters even if those giving or receiving it are unaware of God's presence and activity). If God's action in the world takes place in and through the creatures God has made, as they respond to divine persuasion and realize God's intentions, albeit imperfectly, then this must be true of God's love in particular. God touches us, loves us, through the love we receive from other creatures, and loves other creatures through the love we give.

In addition, whenever you love in a way that acknowledges the one you love as other than yourself, as an independent center of reality and value, whenever you respect the independent moral claim exerted by another self who is a genuine other, you are acknowledging yourself as a creature, and so responding in love to God, whether you realize it or not. Whenever you love in a way that responds to the genuine excellences—beauty, compassion, intelligence, playfulness, strength—of another, you are, again, responding aright to God, since these excellences are reflections and embodiments of God's own perfections. And whenever you love what God loves, as you do whenever you love another person, you are cementing your friendship with God through your alliance with God.

God is the universe's infinite, omnipresent creator, not a part, not a member, of the universe. God doesn't seek to be loved in place of creatures, nor is divine love a substitute for or alternative to creaturely love. We can receive God's love from each other and we can love God as we love each other. Reading the love we give and receive as mediating God's love and as a way of responding aright to God can offer us an additional reason to welcome and celebrate it. To be sure, none of us mediates God's love or embodies God's lovableness with anything like perfection. Still, our fragile and imperfect loves can serve (to muddle the relevant metaphor a bit) as elements of the mustard seed in Jesus' parable: they can play a part, imperfect but real, in healing the brokenness we encounter, in helping to embody God's steadfast and perfect love in the lives of those we touch. When Jacob waits for Rachel, he shares God's love with her and loves God in and through his delight in her. May we find ways to do the same.

53
The Dancing King

David dances. He leaps. He dances with all his might. He dances with an unquenchable passion. The Ark of the Covenant is returning to Jerusalem, and with it a renewed sense of hope and possibility. Israel has interpreted the ark's capture by the Philistines as a sign of divine disfavor. Now, as it comes home, David and his people see new evidence that God is with them. And so they rejoice. And David dances. His response to God is *the body's* response—fluid, dynamic, passionate, sensual. His delight in what he believes God to have done is not expressed in private, in his interior psychic and emotional life; he worships with his body. His worship becomes tangible, visible, in the material world.

Properly understood, the spiritual life *is* material life, life in the world, life in the body. It is not "the flight of the alone to the alone." It is not a matter of what someone does with her or his solitude. David's dancing body is a part of God's good creation, part of the physical life which is God's gift and in and through which we can and must respond to God. He dances to honor the return of a tangible symbol of God's presence to a specific place: to the city of Jerusalem.

The world is part of God's good creation. And so it's good. The whirling form of the ecstatic king is part of creation, is good. The ark is good. The city, David's city, Jerusalem is good. Land matters. Place matters. Bodies matter. David danced. Life in the Spirit is life in the body, life in touch with the material world. But we all know too many stories about the idolatry of this or that place, this or that body, to rest content with the announcement, which may seem troublingly glib, that the material, the tangible, can be a means of grace.

Think of the painful, tortured history of Jerusalem. Continued strife in the eastern Mediterranean only reminds us how much loss, how much violence, how much unresolved conflict can flow from delight in a place identified as in some sense God's. The shared reverence of Muslims, Jews, and Christians for a single city might have been a basis for common worship and deepened understanding. Instead, from the Crusaders to the occupants of today's Jewish West Bank settlements, love for Jerusalem has seemed to entail anything but compassion for those who have shared that love.

Or think of the beauty of the body. Think of David's strong, sleek form glistening in the Jerusalem sun as he danced. Beautiful bodies are worth celebrating, worth enjoying. But think, too, of women abandoned because they lack the lithe bodies of their younger selves. Think of Herodias, craftily using her unsuspecting daughter's dancing form to procure the murder of John the Baptist. Or think of the idolatry of race, which turns a few incidental bodily characteristics into indices of personal value. The body is good. It is part of the good creation. But that is no guarantee that our attitudes toward bodies or the ways in which we use our bodies or those of others will be appropriate. Like places, bodies can be caught up in our idolatry—our tendency to treat a piece of the finite world as if it deserved a deference, wielded an authority, that allowed it to trump the claims of all other elements of reality.

The idolatry of place, the idolatry of the body, the idolatry of what is so clearly good and valuable, are ever-present temptations. They are temptations precisely *because* bodies and places matter. The solution is not to abandon bodies or places. The body is a source of immense and delightful pleasure. Bodies symbolize our personalities and point to our histories, and with them, we touch the lives of others in God's world. Places—like this place, like southern California, which is so dear to me, so integral a part of me—help to sustain our identities, give our lives meaning, tell us who we are.

Psalm 24 provides the beginning of an adequate response. The *whole* earth is God's, says the psalmist—perhaps David himself—"and all that is in it, the world, and those who live in it." Taken to its logical conclusion, the recognition that the whole world is God's must mean that God's presence and activity cannot be localized. If everything is God's, then there are no geographic limits to divine power or divine presence. We cannot simply identify God with any place or object—with the ark by which David dances, or with Jerusalem itself. The *whole* earth is God's, and God is to be found everywhere—not just in

Jerusalem, not just with the ark. To recognize that everything is God's creation, and that God can be encountered everywhere, is to acknowledge that, while each constituent of creation is valuable, none is *ultimate*. Each deserves respect; each deserves to be taken seriously. But no one thing can or should dominate all the others or justify ignoring their reality and value.

Ephesians 1 also suggests something important about our response to the challenge to take bodies and places—God's good gifts—seriously but not ultimately: it speaks of our redemption through the blood of Jesus. We have good reason to be suspicious of any picture of God that shows us a vengeful tyrant being placated by the death of an innocent man; God does not need the death of Jesus or anyone else in order to offer accepting, embracing love. But that does not mean there is nothing healing in that death. Recall that Jesus died, as much as anything, because he resisted the notion that protecting *body* and *place*—an ethnic group and its land—was what mattered most. Many of his contemporaries practiced a "politics of holiness." For them, loyalty to the land and people of Israel meant keeping outsiders at bay and rejecting those whose behavior, ethnicity, or ideology made them different in some way. It meant viewing Greeks and Romans with disdain and marginalizing Jews who didn't fit in. Jesus' ministry was a resounding *no* to such a "politics of holiness." And that *no*, in turn, led him to the cross.

To see God revealed in the life of Jesus is to see his death—occasioned by his opposition to the "politics of holiness"—as an implicit judgment on exclusivism, on the idolatry of a place or of a people whose bodies had something in common. His own brokenness and suffering are pointers to what happens when bodies and places are treated as ultimate in value. To the extent that seeing this can liberate us from the "politics of holiness" that Jesus opposed, can free us *from* self-righteousness and *for* community, can undermine the nagging doubts a scrupulous concern with personal and communal purity can engender about whether we measure up or belong, it is indeed a means of redemption and healing. The mystery of the divine will, says Ephesians 1, is "to gather up all things in . . . [Christ], things in heaven and things on earth." *All things*—all people, all of creation. As if to underscore the inclusiveness of divine grace, Ephesians 3 affirms that "the mystery of Christ" is God's plan to unite Jews and non-Jew in a single community. There is no room in the gospel for exclusion, for the construction of rigid boundaries based on bodies or places.

We can join the psalmist in declaring that all the earth is God's. We can discern in the ministry of Jesus a vision of community characterized by open arms—and in his death a challenge to a different vision of community, one grounded in exclusion and rejection. To find God in all creation and to see God revealed in Jesus is at the same time to recognize the value of the material world, of bodies and places, and to know ourselves called to treat all creatures, not just those to whom we are attached or attracted, with love—at minimum with that love that respectfully acknowledges their dignity, value, and rights, and in some cases with the self-transcending love of devotion. Like David, we can dance. Light of foot, we can delight in the good creation and in God's gifts of particular places, relationships, bodies. But we must also see God in *bodies* other than our own and those whose beauty draws us. We must also see God in *places* other than those where we make our home. We must own the material gifts—the bodies and places we value—as ours in virtue of a grace that embraces *all* bodies, *all* places, *all* people, the whole world.

54
The Glory of God

Imagine the jailer's surprise. The earthquake has opened the doors of the prison. Fearful that the prisoners in his charge have escaped, despairing for his life, he is prepared to kill himself. And then he hears the voice: "Do not harm yourself, for we are all here."

In Luke's story, Paul and Silas have preached to their fellow inmates. They have prayed and sung with them. And they have prevailed upon them to give up their one chance of escape.

Paul's conduct the next morning makes it clear that he is not a milquetoast prepared to suffer injustice uncomplainingly. As a Roman citizen, he makes clear, he has rights. It's not legitimate to imprison him without cause. And he refuses to leave the prison without an apology from the Philippian authorities. Proud man that he is, he wants public vindication. But I think the story also suggests that he knows a prison break might place the jailer in peril and that he chooses not to flee as an act of generosity and compassion. He seeks to liberate from fear, and from Roman punishment.

No doubt his motives are mixed throughout the whole story. Acts 16 says, bluntly, that he heals a slave girl because he is "very much annoyed" at the attention she paid him and Silas. And yet he touches her life with grace, calling her to her right mind. Like the jailer, she is treated with dignity, affirmed, liberated.

In the healing of the slave girl, in Paul's compassion toward the jailer, we see a clear, if perhaps surprising, picture of the glory of God. Perhaps *glory* makes us think of purple robes and brass concerti by Handel and roaring crowds waving lighters. And certainly Christians have always wanted to say that truly to see God is to see what is supremely beautiful, overwhelmingly wonderful and awe-inspiring.

But there are many different ways to see God, many different ways to apprehend the divine beauty and majesty. If we think of divine power as the power of domination, if we envision God as the last of the mediæval emperors, then we may envision divine glory as a consequence of God's ability to dominate and control. Seeing God's glory, then, will be a matter of being overwhelmed by the majesty of a heavenly tyrant. But if God's power is the power of persuasion, if God is vulnerable, suffering love, then perhaps we should look for glory, not in the earthquake, wind, or fire of coercive control but in the still small voice of persuasive empathy. We should expect to see God's glory, not in the suppression of enemies but in their liberation, not in the destruction of the wicked but in their salvation, not in exclusion but in community.

In Psalm 27 it is the delivering, liberating God who is beautiful and glorious. The God who is the recipient of song, who elicits delight, is the God who brings healing and salvation, the God who will never forsake us. Even, says the psalmist, if mother or father should abandon us, God never will. It is in that confidence, that knowledge that we may rest secure in God's love, that our healing, our liberation, consists. God delivers. And it is *as a deliverer, as a healer, as a liberator*, that God is glorious. Thus, Nicholas Lash writes about the crucifixion: "God works *our* beauty in *his* crucifixion, and, in so doing, 'shows' the beauty that is his. In which, with our eyes opened, we may take delight."

In Jesus' prayer in John 17, receiving God's glory leads to complete oneness. As the slave girl is brought into communion with others through her liberation, as the jailer is invited into the Christian family by Paul's concern for his safety, so all persons are to be made one in Christ. To see God as God is, and to know oneself in God, heals us into community. And, in turn, to enter authentic community with each other is precisely to come into right relation with God. Jesus prays that his disciples may see his glory. He has given this glory to the disciples. The upshot of this gift is the oneness of the disciples with each other and with God, which displays God's glory.

Irenaeus once observed that the glory of God was a person fully alive. God's glory does not consist in receiving the adoration of slaves, but in empowering the growth toward maturity of children with authentic freedom and dignity. God's glory is evident when persons are brought into communion with their creator and with each other. God is glorified when humanity's potential is actualized—when we truly love, when we truly flourish. God is glorified when demoniacs are healed, oppressors forgiven, the oppressed delivered, diversity fostered, freedom enhanced, social cooperation extended, community nourished, and creation renewed.

The flourishing of creation truly displays the glory of God. It manifests who God is and what God is like when healing and liberation and fulfillment occur in the world God has made. It is our task to glorify God by healing and enriching the life of God's world.

We seek creation's flourishing when, like Paul and Silas, we offer forgiveness and hope to someone who might expect only hostility and revenge. God's justice is creative—it aims at the creation of wholeness, at the initiation and sustenance of community. Retributive justice may not forgive, but creative justice does. Creative justice emphasizes the creation of new or renewed relationships, not the punishment of the offender. When we are creatively just, we display the glory of God—the God whose grandeur consists not in the ability to coerce but in the capacity to love.

We display that glory when we build loving relationships. In such relationships we offer and experience God's grace. When we love, we are "in" God and God "in" us, as the farewell discourse in John 17 suggests. When I ask forgiveness of someone I love, God's glory is apparent in the asking, in the forgiving, and in the renewed relationship that results. When I help to build a common life for the church in which people are acknowledged and cherished without regard to social class, ethnic background, gender, or sexual orientation, God's glory is made manifest.

We display the divine glory when we serve as agents of God's justice. Psalm 97 declares that God "guards the lives of . . . [the] faithful} and "rescues them from the hand of the wicked." But how is this deliverance accomplished? God works in and through the structures and processes of the created order. When *we* work to enact justice, when God's righteousness is the model for our own, we create new relationships, fashion new forms of community, where God's peace can be displayed. And, in doing so, we display God's glory.

God's glory is often only faintly discerned—in part because God's justice is often at best fitfully present in our lives. God is beautiful, and not merely just; beauty is hardly reducible to moral goodness.

But the failure to see God's beauty is intimately related to the failure to see God's justice. People who cannot see others except in relation to themselves cannot be just, for justice demands an appreciation for the independent reality of the other. But to see others in this way is also to fail to be grasped by their essential beauty, the beauty they have simply because they *are*, the beauty of *being*. And to organize the world around oneself is to be the kind of person who cannot truly see God, and who makes it impossible for others to do so as well.

Because, therefore, human finitude and fallibility impede our perception of God's glory, if we are to see it we must live in hope. And it is to hope, to the hope of an unimpeded communion with God, a complete immersion in the divine glory, that the concluding chapters of the Apocalypse point us. They suggest a direction for our work, and a reason to hope that this work will be fruitful—that loving relationships between persons, between persons and the nonpersonal world, and between persons and God *are* possible. They affirm that loving community is conceivable and achievable, and they invite us into such community: "The Spirit and the bride say, 'Come.' And let everyone who hears say, 'Come.' And let everyone who is thirsty come. Let everyone who wishes take the water of life as a gift" (Apoc. 22:17). Community, creative justice, love—all these are tangible forms of divine grace. As we experience this grace—as we enter deliberately into communion with each other, as we live out of the awareness that we are always in communion with our creator—we truly see the glory of God.

About the Author

GARY CHARTIER is Associate Dean of the Tom and Vi Zapara School of Business and Distinguished Professor of Law and Business Ethics at La Sierra University in Riverside, California. He is the author of books including *Public Practice, Private Law: An Essay on Love, Marriage, and the State* (CUP 2016), *Anarchy and Legal Order: Law and Politics for a Stateless Society* (CUP 2013), *Economic Justice and Natural Law* (CUP 2009), and *The Analogy of Love: Divine and Human Love at the Center of Christian Theology* (Griffin 2017), as well as the co-editor (with Charles W. Johnson) of *Markets Not Capitalism: Individualist Anarchism against Bosses, Inequality, Corporate Power, and Structural Poverty* (Minor Compositions-Autonomedia 2011), (with Chad Van Schoelandt) *The Routledge Handbook of Anarchy and Anarchist Thought* (Routledge 2019), and (with David M. Hart, Ross Miller Kenyon, and Roderick T. Long) *Social Class and State Power* (Palgrave 2018). His byline has appeared over forty times in scholarly journals including *Religious Studies*, the *Anglican Theological Review*, and the *Heythrop Journal*. He is a member of the American Philosophical Association and the Alliance of the Libertarian Left and is a senior fellow and trustee of the Center for a Stateless Society. He has guested on *Reason TV*, *Stossel*, and *The Young Turks with Cenk Uygur*. He has been an active participant in adult religious education and in the delivery of a congregation-driven liturgical worship service for over two decades.

After completing a BA in history and political science at La Sierra (1987, *magna cum laude*), he explored ethics, the philosophy of religion, theology, Christian origins, and political philosophy at the University of Cambridge, receiving a PhD (1991) for a dissertation on the idea of friendship. He graduated with a JD (2001, Order of the Coif) from UCLA, where he studied legal philosophy and public law and qualified for the Judge Jerry Pacht Memorial Award in Constitutional Law. In 2015, he earned an LLD from the University of Cambridge for his work in legal philosophy. He is a proud southern California native who wishes he had attended UC Sunnydale. Visit him on-line at <http://www.garychartier.net>.

www.ingramcontent.com/pod-product-compliance
Lightning Source LLC
Chambersburg PA
CBHW061318040426
42444CB00011B/2706